CLOUDS OF THE LORD AND BIBLE PROPHECY

proof of mankind's interaction with god

W. T. Ness

ISBN: 0648243303
ISBN 13: 9780648243304

CONTENTS

What are these clouds that have visited humanity throughout the Bible? *Clouds of the Lord* will help you to understand what has happened in the past, give you some understanding of the present, and help you finally understand the future. *Clouds of the Lord* is a key to unlocking the mysteries in the Bible. It's not the only key, but it is a very important one.

Key Words

Clouds or *clouds of the Lord* seem to be vehicles of energy or surrounded by energy.

Fire by night and *Chariots of God* are other terms for these vehicles.

Tabernacle is the word for a tent.

CHAPTER 1
OLD TESTAMENT

Clouds (vehicles) have visited humans throughout the ages, including visiting Moses in Exodus 24:15: "And Moses went up the mountain, and a cloud covered the mountain. And the glory of the Lord abode upon Mount Sinai, and the cloud covered it six days, and the seventh day God called to Moses from the cloud. And the sight of the glory of the Lord was like fire on the top of the mountain to the eyes of the children of Israel. And Moses went into the midst of the cloud, and was there forty days and forty nights."

The Old Testament prophecy Isaiah 19 says, "The burden of Egypt, behold the Lord rides upon a swift cloud and shall come into Egypt."

And even Jesus Christ. Acts 1:9–11 says, "And when Jesus had spoken these things [to proclaim the Gospel throughout the planet] while they looked, he was taken up into the sky, and a cloud received him [the ascension of Christ]."

The occupants of these clouds were witnessed and recorded inadvertently in the Bible, and they reveal the future of humanity. The amazing predictions in the Bible show we are in the final generation of humanity before these beings set up a worldwide government in order to prevent humanity from annihilating itself.

Check and prove to yourself that the information written here is true and accurate, and if it is, make a decision about what you will do with your life. The wars you see now throughout the world (the Arab Spring, the War on Terror, etc.) will end up bringing the armies of the world to the Middle East, where they will attack Jesus Christ, who will be returning in the clouds of the Lord (see Joel 3;2, Zechariah 14;2, Luke 21;20). The world's armies will be destroyed, according to the Bible, ushering in world peace for one thousand years. Have you ever heard this? This is one of the most astounding revelations in the Bible, but you don't hear this mentioned in most of the world's churches. Isaiah 46:10 says, "I am God and there is none like me, Declaring the end from the beginning, and from ancient times things not yet done, saying, 'My counsel shall stand, and I will accomplish all my purpose.'"

Daniel 2:28 says, "But there is a God in heaven who reveals mysteries."

Can this be true? Can there really be a God who declares events from ancient times about the future?

Read on, and find out. This book provides comfort for those who have lost loved ones. The Bible describes a wonderful future, when those who are alive will be reunited with their loved ones who are sleeping (dead) in what is called *the second resurrection,* which is described as a time of great joy.

But first the prophecies in the Bible that have not occurred yet will have to come to pass.

This book contains information that was not previously available and is written to give people an understanding of the past, present, and future that will make the difficult times ahead more bearable.

The Bible is a collection of books written about events and interactions with beings who claim to serve the creator of the entire universe, who states he has a fantastic purpose for his creation (humanity).

People as diverse as fishermen to kings have written the Bible, which has been translated and interpreted (and often misinterpreted) about events over thousands of years. The basis of three of the world's largest religions—Judaism, Christianity, and Islam, with all their differing branches—has an impact on the entire world's population.

Many books are currently available that belittle this book of books (the Bible); they are written by supposedly intelligent men who are not only university educated but who teach at some of the world's leading universities as well.

This book is in response to these misleading books and for the average person who wants some real answers. Is there a loving creator God or not? Is there a future beyond the grave? Is there hope beyond death?

This book is to impart some knowledge to people who are humble enough to investigate whether its contents are true or not, and it will give some real hope.

The Bible (when it's correctly understood) shows a consistency in its statements that will make any logically thinking person believe it's based on true events.

The incredible revelation of the clouds of the Lord is only one area of the consistency of the Bible, which was written about events that happened some thirty-five hundred years ago as well as events that will happen in the near future, when the entire world will witness these clouds again at the second coming of Jesus Christ.

Do not let other people (myself included) make up your mind for you, no matter what university they teach at or how many books they have written belittling the Bible. One very famous scientist who is otherwise brilliant said, "A future beyond the grave is a fairy tale for those afraid of death, and that when the brain finally dies there is no future hope."

3

This book (*Clouds of the Lord*) and the *fairy tale* it reveals will give you some real hope, for it is a key to understanding that these supposedly wise men have not found.

Read this book, investigate what it says, and then make up your own mind.

CHAPTER 2

IS THERE PROOF OF THE EXISTENCE OF GOD?

Have you ever wondered whether God is real? Does the Bible contain unbiased evidence of such?

What if you came across information that is conclusive? Would you reject it because it does not fit in with your current belief system?

Evidence has always been there but has not been recognized till now. Study this book in its entirety. If you humbly do so, your life will begin to change, and you will see the world differently.

What is written here is proof of the existence of much higher beings than humans, and it has been here all along.

Isn't belief in God something that has been disproved by modern science? Isn't it intellectually superior to believe that only primitive (or stupid) people believe in God and the Bible in today's modern world? Is that what you think?

This book will provide consistent evidence that the Bible is correct when it says in Psalm 14:1, "The fool says there is no God." The self-declared intellectually superior modern militant atheist movement the "brights" such as Richard Dawkins and others who write books ridiculing the Bible. Make up your own mind; don't let these people (the militant atheists) dictate what is true and what is false to you.

You have the intelligence to do this if you are able to read this page. Follow the evidence where it leads very carefully, and don't trust anyone else; investigate yourself. Believe the evidence.

There are books and Internet sites that state the Bible is nothing more than a collection of primitive myths and legends with no more merit than other ancient tales put together by Bronze and Iron Age individuals. This book will show that these Bronze and Iron Age individuals were guided by beings much more advanced than humanity is today. The so-called Bible experts have been miseducated at universities that have little real idea of the meaning of the Bible. This book shows the real story of the Bible, which cannot be taught by atheists. A closed mind cannot take in accurate information. Biblical prophecy (although difficult to understand, the Bible itself states that God blocks arrogant people from understanding it) shows the authenticity of the Bible. The Bible states it provides prophecy so those who accept God know he exists and is in control. No other work in history shows such accurate and detailed prophecy covering thousands of years.

The beings who visit us in the clouds of the Lord come from the creator of the entire universe, who has created us in his image so that we'll ultimately join him as sons and daughters and heirs of the universe. (At least that is where the evidence leads.)

The writer first saw one of these clouds at the age of fifteen. At the time, he had no idea what he had witnessed.

This will reveal more and more as we move toward our destiny.

This book is honest. The writer will not include anything he does not believe to be true for fame or fortune. The most important thing in God's mind for his creation is love, according to the Bible. Love is above knowledge, but the Bible also states in Hosea

4:6 that "my people perish for lack of knowledge." So if you don't have knowledge, what can happen?

I hope to instill some of God's knowledge (if he exists) to those who humbly desire it and find true fulfillment in life before I die.

CHAPTER 3

TIME PERIOD: 1900 BC

In Genesis 15, four hundred years before Moses, God tells Abram (also known as Abraham) that his descendants will be as numerous as the stars. Abraham asks God how he will know this will happen, and Abraham sacrifices some animals, which was a common practice in his time (human sacrifice was also commonplace).

At night, something appears to Abraham that looks like a smoking furnace and a burning lamp, and it moves between the sacrificed animals. That day God tells Abraham he will give the land between the Nile River in Egypt and the Euphrates River in Iraq to his descendants.

Abraham has a son named Ishmael with his Egyptian slave, Hagar. This child is considered today by those in the Arabic and Islamic worlds to be their forefather. And years later at the age of ninety-nine, Abraham has a child with his Hebrew wife, Sarah.

God tells Abraham he will give the land of Canaan to his son, Isaac. Canaan is the area we refer to today as Israel, where the Jewish nation now lives.

The sons of Ishmael, the Arabs, and the sons of Isaac, the Jews, live in the area between the Nile and Euphrates Rivers today. The

Arabs claim Abraham as an ancestor through Ishmael, and the Jews claim Abraham is their ancestor through Isaac.

The Bible stated nearly four thousand years ago that Abraham would be the father of many nations.

A smoking furnace and a burning lamp, and then God made a covenant with Abraham that has come to pass (Abraham is known as the father of many nations).

Ancient man's descriptions of being visited by a higher intelligence. Read on, and make up your own mind.

CHAPTER 4

TIME PERIOD: 1490 BC

About thirty-five hundred years ago, God empowered Moses to bring the descendants of Isaac (the twelve tribes of Israel) out of Egypt and back to the Promised Land (modern-day Israel), which he had promised to Abraham and Isaac and Isaac's son, Israel (also known as Jacob), hundreds of years previously.

The Israelites left slavery in Egypt after God won the contests against Egypt's so-called gods. The last contest ended in the deaths of the Egyptians' firstborn sons; an event that the Jews and some Christian churches still celebrate today as the Passover: the destroyer passed over the houses of the Israelites and only killed the Egyptians (Exod. 12–14).

> This day you shall keep as a memorial; you shall keep this feast to the Lord throughout your generations; you shall keep it as a feast forever; when your children ask you what is the meaning of this feast, you shall say, "It is the Lord's Passover," who passed over the houses of the children of Israel in Egypt when he killed the Egyptians.

About 3,500 years later, the Passover is still being told and celebrated. The Israelites left Egypt after being there for 430 years.

The first mention of clouds (or energy vehicles, spaceships, interdimensional craft, etc.) is in Exodus 13–21: approximately thirty-five hundred years ago on the main Egyptian side of the Red Sea.

> And the Lord went before them by day in a pillar of a cloud, to lead them the way, and by night in a pillar of fire, to give them light to go by day and night.

Obviously this is not a rain cloud but simple ancient humanity's description of an extraterrestrial craft, much like a child today might describe a helicopter looking similar to a cloud in daylight and to a fire at night, since it produces its own light energy.

The Egyptian army pursued the Israelites and caught up with them at the sea. Exodus 14:19 says, "And the angel of God, which went before the camp of Israel, removed and went behind them, and the pillar of the cloud went from before their face, and stood behind them, and it came between the camp of the Egyptians and the camp of Israel, and it was a cloud and darkness to them, but it gave light by night, so they came not to each other all the night." In this passage, the angel of God prevents the Egyptian army from slaughtering the Israelites.

Exodus 14:21 says, "And Moses stretched out his hand over the sea, and the Lord caused the sea to go back by a strong east wind all that night and made the sea dry land, and the waters were divided." The sea slowly parted all night, not quickly as depicted in movies, and was quite possibly held back by a force field from the cloud (or energy vehicle).

Exodus 14:22 says, "And the Israelites went into the midst of the sea on dry land, and the waters were a wall unto them on their right hand and on their left hand."

Atheists try to claim this description in the Bible was a result of the Santorini explosion thirty-six hundred years ago, which is believed to have destroyed the Minoan civilization. It's funny how the water parted and just stayed there, and the Israelites walked through the towering sea underneath the cloud (1 Cor. 10:1). These clouds and lights interact with the Israelites for eighteen hundred years and are prophesied by Jesus Christ that he will return in these clouds (Rev. 1:7)

And the Egyptians pursued the Israelites and went in after them into the midst of the sea—all pharaoh's horses, his chariots, and his horsemen. (The ancient Egyptians believed pharaoh was a god.)

> And it came to pass, in the morning light, the Lord looked upon the Egyptians through the pillar of fire and the cloud and caused the wheels to come off the chariots, which terrified the Egyptians. God then told Moses to wave his staff at the waters and the sea, and the waters then collapsed on the pursuing Egyptians, drowning them. (The force field was likely removed.)

Then Moses and the Israelites sang this song to the Lord: "And with a blast of your nostrils [from the cloud] the waters were gathered together, the waters stood upright like a heap, the enemy [the Egyptians] said we will overtake them and slaughter them, you blew with your wind and the sea covered them, who is like unto thee, O Lord, among the gods."

Fifteen hundred years later, the apostle Paul wrote in his letter to the church in Corinth (1 Cor. 10:1): "Moreover brethren, I don't want you to be ignorant, that all our fathers [ancestors who left Egypt with Moses] were under the cloud [energy vehicle] and they all passed through the sea [on dry land with the waters standing up high on their right and their left]." I also don't want you to be ignorant of this fact that all religious leaders and atheists have missed this and are ignorant. And they were all baptized with Moses in the cloud and in the sea. Let's have a good think here. No movie or religion I have ever heard of talks about or shows this event about the Israelites passing through the sea underneath a cloud. Religious leaders and filmmakers talk about or show Moses parting the sea in moments, which are contrary to the Bible's description of it being parted by "a strong east wind all night." And they make no mention of the cloud being above the Israelites as they passed through the sea. Why? Because they have not understood the cloud or its relevance throughout the Bible.

Paul (who was previously persecuting the followers of Jesus Christ, being involved in their imprisonment and even executions on behalf of the Jewish leaders) became a Christian himself when on the way to Syria.

Acts 9:3 says, "And as he came near to Damascus, suddenly, a light from heaven shone round about him, and a voice from the light said to him, 'Saul [Paul] why do you persecute me?' Paul replies, 'Who are you?' Then the voice from the light says, I am Jesus, and tells Paul to continue on to Damascus and he will be told what to do there." Clouds from heaven, lights from heaven, and other similar descriptions are included throughout the Bible.

Then a few months later, the Israelites complained against Moses and his older brother, Aaron, over a lack of food, and Moses told them that in the morning they would see the glory of the Lord with the cloud and that they would have bread to eat in the morning and meat to eat in the evening.

And it came to pass as Aaron spoke to the whole congregation of the children of Israel that they looked toward the wilderness, and the glory of the Lord appeared in the cloud.

And it came to pass in the evening that quail came and covered the camp, and in the morning, dew lay around the host of the Israelites.

And when the dew was gone, there was a small round thing on the ground, and Moses told them it was the bread God had promised.

Moses told the Israelites to fill an omer with the bread (manna from heaven), keep it to show their future generations, and tell them how God fed them in the wilderness when he brought them out of Egypt.

Three months later, God called Moses up to Mount Sinai and told him to tell the Israelites that you have seen what I did to the Egyptians, now if you will obey me and keep my covenant, I will make you a holy nation.

And you shall be unto me a kingdom of priests, these are the words you shall speak to the Israelites.
And all the people answered and said, "All that God has spoken we will do."
And Moses returned the words of the Israelites to God.
God said to Moses, "I will come to you in a cloud [energy vehicle], and the people will hear when I speak with you, and believe you forever." (Exod. 19:9)

Thirty-five hundred years later, people still believe Moses. The three main religions of the world, Christianity, Judaism, and Islam, all accept Moses as God's prophet.

In Exodus 19:11, God tells Moses to prepare the Israelites for the third day when God will come down in the sight of all the Israelites upon Mount Sinai.

Exodus 19:17–18 says, "And Moses brought forth the people out of the camp to meet with God, and they stood at the nether parts of the mountain, and Mount Sinai was full of smoke because God descended upon it in fire." In Exodus 19:19, Moses speaks, and God answers him with his voice.

Exodus 19:20 tells us that the Lord came down on the top of Mount Sinai and called Moses up to the top of the mountain, and when Moses went up, God told him that only he and his brother, Aaron, were to come up Mount Sinai to him. So Moses went down the mountain to the Israelites and spoke to them.

Exodus 20:2 says, "I am the Lord thy God, who brought you out of Egypt, out of slavery, out of the house of bondage and says you are to have no other gods besides me" and tells the Israelites the Ten Commandments. (Many of the world's laws throughout history stem from these commandments.)

And the Lord says to Moses, "Come up to me into the mountain and wait there, and I will give you tablets of stone, with a law and commandments which I have written [on the stone tablets] that you may teach them to the Israelites."

And Moses went up into the mountain, and a cloud covered the mountain, and the glory of the Lord abode on Mount Sinai, and the cloud (energy vehicle) covered it for six days, and on the seventh day, God called to Moses out of the midst of the cloud (energy vehicle).

And the sight of the glory of the Lord was like devouring fire on top of the mountain in the eyes of all the Israelites.

Exodus 24:18 says, "And Moses went into the midst of the cloud," meaning that Moses went into the energy vehicle. Fifteen hundred years later, Moses visited Jesus Christ, also in one of these clouds. The event when Jesus went into the cloud before his death and then was taken away by a cloud after his resurrection is known as the Transfiguration of Christ. Acts 1:9 says, "And when he had spoken these things a cloud took him from their sight." Then the angels told the apostles that Jesus would come back the same way, in these clouds (Acts 1:11).

Moses stayed in the cloud (energy vehicle) on top of Mount Sinai for forty days and forty nights, during which time he was instructed to build the tabernacle and the ark of the covenant.

After the forty days in the cloud, God told Moses to go back down the mountain to the Israelites, saying your people have corrupted themselves, and have made a golden calf, and sacrificed unto it and worshipped it, saying this is our god who brought us up out of Egypt.

And Moses went down the mountain with the tablets of stone Exodus 32:15 (the Ten Commandments), and when he saw the golden calf, he threw the tablets and broke them and threw the golden calf into the fire. Moses built the tabernacle (the tent for meeting with God), and Moses could then visit God in the tabernacle.

And it came to pass that as Moses entered into the tabernacle, the cloudy pillar descended and stood at the door of the tabernacle, and the Lord talked with Moses. Once again, God came down in the cloudy pillar.

And all the people saw the cloudy pillar stand at the tabernacle door, and all the people rose up and worshipped, every man in his tent door. And the Lord spoke to Moses face-to-face, as a man speaks to a friend.

A being made of energy talked face-to-face with the human Moses. And the Lord told Moses to make two tablets of stone like the first ones he had broken, and God would write on the tablets all the words that were on the first ones. And God told Moses to be ready in the morning to come up to Mount Sinai with the tablets.

And Moses rose up early in the morning and went up on to Mount Sinai with the two tablets "and the Lord descended in the cloud" (energy vehicle) (Exod. 34:5) and stood with Moses there. A cloud coming from heaven with God inside it—does this sound like a rain cloud? These clouds are mentioned throughout the Bible and also described as chariots.

And Moses stayed inside the cloud from heaven for another forty days and nights, and when he came down from Mount Sinai with the Ten Commandments, his face shone, and the people were afraid to come close to him.

Moses put a veil on his face and told the Israelites what God had said to him on Mount Sinai. Moses took the veil off when he went into the tabernacle to speak with God (who appeared above the mercy seat where God would appear in a cloud) and put it back on when he came out to speak with the people.

Exodus 40:33 says, "So Moses finished the work [setting up the ark of the covenant in the finished tent of the congregation]. Then a cloud [energy vehicle] covered the tent of the congregation, and the glory of the Lord filled the tabernacle [God inspected his finished tabernacle]. And Moses was unable to enter the tent because the cloud [energy vehicle] abode upon it and the glory of the Lord filled it," similar to 1 Kings 8.

In 1000 BC, nearly five hundred years later, God told Solomon, the son of King David (from the story of David and Goliath), to build his temple and put the ark of the covenant in it.

And once again, five hundred years after Moses lived, the cloud came again. And it came to pass that when the priests came out of the holy place, the cloud filled the house of the Lord (God inspected his temple) so that the priests could not stand to minister because of the cloud, for the glory of the Lord had filled the house of the Lord.

So here we have the cloud coming to the finished temple and the glory of the Lord filling it.

Two almost-identical events happened five hundred years apart: God came to inspect his finished tabernacle in Moses's time in the wilderness, and God came to visit his temple in Jerusalem in King Solomon's time.

The ancient Israelites witnessed awesome power in these clouds, and King David recorded it in song in Psalm 68 to the chief musician, to him who rides the heavens of heavens, which were of old. God's strength is in the clouds, a reference to these energy vehicles.

And when the cloud (energy vehicle) was taken up from the tabernacle, the children of Israel went onward, following the cloud in all their journeys. But when the cloud did not rise up, they stayed in one place till the day the cloud did rise up. By now it should be obvious that these are not rain clouds but vehicles composed of or covered with light energy.

Psalm 68 says, "The chariots [vehicles of God] are twenty thousand, and thousands of angels, the Lord is among them, as in Sinai, in the holy place."

Exodus 40 says, "For the cloud of the Lord [energy vehicle] was upon the tabernacle by day, and fire [light] was on it by night, in the sight of the house of Israel, throughout all their journeys."

Hundreds of thousands of people followed a cloud for forty years. The cloud was not your regular rain cloud, that's for sure, and the fire was the way the cloud appeared at night.

CHAPTER 5
BOOK OF NUMBERS

N umbers is the fourth book of Moses, covering the forty years in the wilderness.

Numbers 9 says, "And on the day the tabernacle was taken up, the cloud [energy vehicle] covered the tabernacle. Namely the tent of testimony, [containing the ark of the covenant and the law, the Ten Commandments], and at evening there was upon the tabernacle the appearance of fire [the light energy emanating from the energy vehicle in the dark] until the morning". Similar to a light bulb being switched on in the night and in the daylight.

Numbers 9:16 says that the cloud covered the tent by day and had the appearance of fire by night.

And when the cloud was taken up from the tabernacle, after that, the children of Israel journeyed, and in the place where the cloud abode (stopped), the Israelites pitched their tents.

Following this cloud? Pitching their tents when the cloud stopped? A rain cloud? Not very likely.

At the commandment of the Lord (when the cloud, or energy vehicle, rose up off the tabernacle), the Israelites journeyed, and at the commandment of the Lord (when the cloud stopped), they pitched their tents.

As long as the cloud abode on the tabernacle (the tent of meeting with God where the ark of the covenant and the Ten Commandments were stored), the Israelites rested in their tents.

And when the cloud stayed on the tabernacle for many days, the children of Israel followed God's command and did not continue their journey.

And when the cloud was a few days on the tabernacle, according to the commandment of the Lord, they journeyed not.

And so it was, when the cloud abode from the evening until the morning, and when the cloud rose up in the morning, then they resumed their journey, whether it was by day or by night that the cloud rose up off the tent, they resumed their journey.

Hundreds of thousands of men, women, children, and animals followed this cloud through the Desert of Sinai. Whether it was for two days, a month, or a year that the cloud stayed on the tabernacle, the Israelites stayed in their tents, but when it rose up off the tent, they journeyed, following it.

What sort of cloud commands such devotion?

At the commandment of the Lord, they stayed in their tents. And at the commandment of the Lord, they journeyed.

They kept the charge of the Lord (they obeyed), at the commandment of the Lord, by the hand of Moses.

Numbers 10:11 says, "And it came to pass on the twentieth day of the second month, in the second year [after leaving Egypt] that the cloud rose up from the tabernacle, and the children of Israel took their journeys out of the wilderness of Sinai, and the cloud rested in the wilderness of Paran. And the cloud of the Lord was upon them by day when they went out of the camp.

And Moses went out and told the people the words of the Lord and gathered seventy men of the elders of Israel and set them around the tabernacle.

And the Lord came down in a cloud." What sort of cloud does God come down in? Humans can come down in helicopters, hot air balloons, helium airships, planes, and so on, but these clouds are well past our current levels of human technology. And the Israelites were describing them thirty-five hundred years ago.

And the Lord spoke to Moses and took of the spirit that was upon him and gave it to the seventy elders.

In Numbers 12, Miriam and Aaron (Moses's older brother and sister) spoke against Moses because of the Ethiopian woman he had married, and they said, "Has God only spoken to Moses, has he not spoken to us also, and the Lord heard it. And the Lord spoke suddenly to Moses, to Aaron and to Miriam."

Come out you three to the tabernacle of the congregation, and they came out.

And the Lord came down in the pillar of the cloud (a pillar coming down from the cloud is an energy vehicle) and stood in the door of the tabernacle and called Aaron and Miriam.

And they both came forward, and God said, "Hear my words if there be a prophet among you, I, the Lord will make myself known to him in a vision, and will speak to him in a dream.

Not so with my servant Moses, with him I will speak face to face, and the similitude of the Lord shall he behold.

And the anger of the Lord was kindled against them and he departed. And the cloud with the Lord God inside departed off the tabernacle and behold Miriam became leprous, white as snow, and Aaron looked upon Miriam and she was leprous."

In Numbers 14, the Israelites reached Kadesh-barnea (in southern modern-day Israel), and spies reported the inhabitants of the land were giants and lived in well-fortified cities.

The Israelites complained and said, "Why has God brought us into this land to die by the sword, and our wives and children should be prey for the giants?Is it not better for us to return to Egypt?"

And they said to each other, "Let's choose a captain to return us to Egypt."

Joshua and Caleb stated that the land ahead was exceedingly good, and they told the Israelites not to rebel against God. Then the Israelites talked about stoning Joshua and Caleb, and once again, the glory of the Lord appeared in the tabernacle of the congregation before all the children of Israel.

Then God said to Moses that he would destroy the Israelites and make Moses himself a great nation.

Moses pleaded with God to pardon the Israelites' lack of faith, and Moses said to the Lord, "Then the Egyptians shall hear of [the destruction of the Israelites] for you brought up this people with your might from among them. The plagues God brought upon Egypt and the destruction of the Egyptian army in the sea.

And they will tell it to the inhabitants of this land, for they have heard you are God, and you are among this people. That you, Lord, are seen face to face. And your cloud stands over them and goes before them, by day in a pillar of cloud and by night in a pillar of fire."

Moses described the energy vehicle that traveled with the Israelites. To the ancient Israelites, it looked like a cloud in the daytime, and at night its light energy made it look like fire. It emanated light like a lightbulb when switched on in the daytime, and then it was highly illuminated at night when it dissipated the darkness.

The cloud and fire moved through the sky in a controlled manner.

We could mimic cloud and fire today with a helicopter and fool some of the world's most primitive natives, such as some of the people who live in the Amazon who would think the helicopter was from a god.

Moses said to God, "If you destroy all these people, then the nations which have heard of your fame will speak, saying, 'Because the Lord was not able to bring this people unto the land he swore unto them, therefore he has slain them in the wilderness.'"

God said to Moses, "I have pardoned them according to your request, but as surely as I live, because all these men have seen my glory and my miracles which I did in Egypt and in the wilderness, they will not see [the holy land] which I swore to their ancestors, but you shall wander in the wilderness for forty years, but your little ones, the ones you said would be prey unto the inhabitants of the land, they I will bring into the land which you despised."

Twenty years later, Korah, Dathan, and Abiram contested Moses's and Aaron's positions as leaders of the Israelites. Numbers 16 says, "And Korah gathered all the congregation against them unto the door of the tabernacle of the congregation and the glory of the Lord once again appeared to all the congregation."

And God said to Moses, Numbers 16:32: "Separate from those who are against you and Aaron." Then God opened the earth, and the rebels were swallowed up; those with Korah all fell down into the pit, and the earth closed over them, and they all perished. And it came to pass when the congregation was gathered against Moses and Aaron, they looked toward the tabernacle of the congregation, and the cloud again covered the tent, and the glory of the Lord appeared.

The Israelites arrived at the Desert of Zin and complained about a lack of water, and Moses and Aaron went from the assembly of the complaining Israelites to the door of the tabernacle of the congregation, and the glory of the Lord appeared to them, and the Lord spoke to Moses: "Gather the assembly together, you and your brother Aaron and speak to a rock before their eyes, and it shall give water for them all to drink." Moses assembled the people and hit the rock twice, and water came out abundantly for the Israelites to drink.

Then Moses sent messengers to the kings of Edom and told them to say, "And when we cried out to the Lord, he heard our voice and sent his angel, and he has brought us out of Egypt." The Israelites had been in Egypt for 430 years. Moses also said, "And

behold we are in Kadesh, a city in the utmost parts of your border."
Complemented by Exodus 23:20: "Behold I send an angel before
you to keep you in the way and to bring you to the place I have pre-
pared for you [the Holy Land], beware of him and obey his voice,
provoke him not for he will not pardon your transgressions."

God told the Israelites to obey his angel in a cloud, and he would
take them to the holy land that he had promised to Abraham,
Isaac, and Jacob (also known as Israel). They carried with them the
ark of the covenant with the Ten Commandments and the bones
of Joseph inside the ark.

CHAPTER 6
DEUTERONOMY

Deuteronomy is the fifth book of Moses—Moses's parting counsel and death at 120 years of age.

It was about 1450 BC.

The Lord, your God, who goes before you, shall fight for you, the same as he did for you in Egypt before your eyes (God visited plagues on Egypt, which the gods of Egypt were unable to prevent, and destroyed the Egyptian army in the sea).

And Moses told the assembly (most of whom were born in the wilderness in the last forty years since leaving Egypt) how God supported the hundreds of thousands of Israelites in the preceding forty years in the wilderness, providing bread (manna), meat (quail), and water. And God went before the Israelites in what looked to them like fire by night a cloud by day to search out a place for them to pitch their tents.

Now Moses warned the new generation: take heed to yourselves, lest you forget the things your eyes have seen, but teach them to your sons, and your sons' sons.

Especially the day you stood before the Lord in Horeb, when the Lord said to me, "Gather the people together, and I will make them hear my words, that they may learn to obey me all the days they live upon the earth, and that they may teach their children."

Almost thirty-five years later, children are still being taught about these events. It's no coincidence that through the big three—Judaism, Christianity, and Islam—half the world's population is learning about these events, and the other half is quickly being taught now also.

Deuteronomy 4:11 says, "And you came near and stood under the mountain, and the mountain burned with fire, clouds and darkness, and the Lord spoke to you out of the midst of the fire [the same as Moses and the burning bush] you heard the voice, but you saw no one, only you heard the voice" (Moses saw the Lord's likeness as he spoke face to face).

And God declared to you his covenant, the Ten Commandments, which he wrote on two tablets of stone. Take heed unto yourself that you saw no likeness on the day that the Lord spoke to you in Horeb out of the midst of the fire (energy vehicle).

So don't corrupt yourself and make an image again (like the golden calf). Hundreds of thousands of men, women, and children heard a booming voice coming from the cloud (energy vehicle) in the daytime and the appearance of fire at night.

> Take heed to yourselves, lest you forget the covenant of the Lord your God, which he made with you.
> I call heaven and earth to witness against you this day that the Lord shall scatter you among the nations, and you shall be left few in number among the heathen, where the Lord shall lead you (Deut. 4:26)

History attests to this scattering among the nations happening: in about 730 BC, ten of the tribes were taken into captivity by the Assyrian Empire and then were lost to general history. History refers to them as the ten lost tribes of Israel.

The remaining tribes, known as the Jews, resisted the Assyrians and were finally taken into captivity by the Babylonians under King Nebuchadnezzar in southern Iraq.

When the Babylonian Empire fell to the Medes and Persians in 539 BC, the Persian king Cyrus the Great allowed any Jew who wished to return to Jerusalem and rebuild God's temple there. (See the "Edict of Cyrus.")

This was followed by the Greek invasion of the Persian Empire under Alexander the Great two hundred years later. The Bible clearly predicted the Greeks conquering the Persian Empire; when Alexander the Great came to Jerusalem, the religious authorities showed him the prophecies that said the king of the Greeks would come, and they turned the city over to him without fighting.

The Roman Empire had control of the holy land at the time of Jesus Christ (this was also prophesied to happen), and following numerous rebellions by the Jews, the Romans ultimately decreed "that any Jew setting foot in Jerusalem [the Romans renamed it Aelia Capitolia] would be put to death in the second century."

The Jews were scattered among nearly all the nations on earth; this event is called the Jewish Diaspora. The Jews have at different times been expelled from many nations in the world—England, France, Spain, Portugal, Russia, Germany under the Nazis and Adolf Hitler (whose empire was also prophesied). The Nazis performed the Holocaust, the greatest destruction of the Jews ever.

Now the Arabs and Muslims have taken on the role of trying to destroy the Jews.

The Jews resettled in Palestine under the UN Partition Plan of 1947 after the World War II, and the UN plan was rejected by the Arabs, who launched an all-out attack on the fledgling Jewish state after the British withdrew their troops. Today Israel is the homeland of most of the world's Jews.

Deuteronomy 4:33 says, "Did ever people hear the voice of God speaking out of the midst of the fire as you have heard and lived?

Out of heaven [the cloud and fire in the sky], he made you hear his voice that he might instruct you, and upon the earth he showed you his great fire, and you heard his words out of the midst of the fire."

Much like a primitive race today would view events if a helicopter addressed them with a loudspeaker in the day, and the bright light at night, only there were no helicopters thirty-five hundred years ago.

In Deuteronomy 10:1, Moses told the new generation that forty years earlier, God had said to make two stone tablets like the first tablets that Moses had broken, and God had asked Moses to come up the mountain to him.

Moses went up the mountain, and the Lord wrote the Ten Commandments on the new tablets, and Moses came down the mountain and put the tablets into the wooden ark he had built (the ark of the covenant).

When Moses was 120 years old, God said he would die. In Genesis 6:3, 120 years is the age set by God for man: "Man's days shall be limited to 120." A Harvard University also acknowledges that the upper limit for a human life-span seems to be 120. Moses commands the priests—the Levites—to place God's law in the ark of the covenant and tells them to read the law aloud to the Israelites every seven years.

Once again God appears in the tabernacle in a "pillar from the cloud, over the door of the tabernacle, and God tells Moses after his death, the Israelites will rise up and go whoring after the other gods of the people of the land [Canaan] and break the covenant they have with God."

Moses died at 120 years, and Joshua led the Israelites over the Jordan River into the Promised Land.

The next mention of Moses with the clouds is fifteen hundred years later, when Moses met Jesus in a cloud in AD 32. In Luke 9:27, Jesus took three of his disciples—Peter, John, and James—and went up a mountain to pray. And as they prayed, his countenance was altered, and his raiment became white and glistening. And Moses and Elijah, who appeared in glory (as resurrected beings), talked with Jesus. They had lived and died fifteen hundred and one thousand years previously, and they spoke of his coming death by crucifixion in Jerusalem.

But Peter and the others with him were heavy with sleep, and when they woke, they saw his glory and the two men who stood with him.

"And it came to pass as they departed from him, Peter said to Jesus, "Master, it is good for us to be here; let us make three tents, one for you, one for Moses, and one for Elijah." Have you ever heard this before?

Jesus meeting the resurrected Moses and Elijah? The disciples seeing for themselves what Jesus stated—that some of his disciples would see God's kingdom? And now? Then once again nearly fifteen hundred years after the death of Moses, while Peter spoke, the cloud comes again, and overshadows them, and they were fearful as Jesus, Moses, and Elijah went into the cloud (energy vehicle). And there came a voice out of the cloud, saying, "This is my beloved son; listen to him."

God the creator, father, told Peter, John, and James that Jesus was his son from the cloud, which Jesus, the resurrected Moses, and Elijah had just entered.

"And when the voice and cloud were gone, they saw Jesus alone." God brought Moses and Elijah to meet Jesus in this energy vehicle, which is described as a cloud throughout the Bible. Similar accounts are in the books of Matthew and Mark later described in this book, but they are not exactly the same, showing no evidence of collusion to deceive people.

This brings us to the end of the books of Moses but certainly not to the end of the interactions of the clouds of the Lord.

It shows the continuing involvement of the clouds of the Lord in the times of the prophets who followed Moses till Jesus Christ came. The clouds of the Lord also had interactions with Jesus. Reading and understanding this book will help open up more of the Bible to those who want some real answers. Is there truth in the Bible, or is it just silly fairy tales written by Bronze and Iron Age humans? To get a full understanding of the clouds of the Lord, all of this book must be studied, researched, and proven to be accurate. This book contains information from Old Testament prophets such as Daniel, Samuel, Jeremiah, Isaiah, Ezekiel, Nehemiah, and others. It also contains information from King David, King Solomon, and others. This book will surprise you because this has not been seen before; the answer is that this information has been sealed up till the last days, as the book of Daniel says. What you do with this information is your affair. You can take this on board and decide to change your life and become a more giving person, in line with what the creator desires, or you can ignore it.

CHAPTER 7

THE BOOK OF KINGS, 1000 BC

And it came to pass in the four hundred and eightieth year after the children of Israel came out of the land of Egypt, in the fourth year of Solomon's reign over Israel, in the fourth month of Zif, which is the second month, that Solomon began to build the house of the Lord, the temple in Jerusalem. First Kings 6 states that in the eleventh year of his reign, in the month Bul, was the house of the Lord finished, throughout all its parts, and according to all its fashion (1 Kings 6:1)

So was Solomon seven years building the temple of God. So was ended all the work that King Solomon made for the house of the Lord, and Solomon brought all the things that David (David and Goliath) his father had dedicated. Silver and gold and the vessels, he put among the treasures of the house of the Lord.

Then Solomon assembled the elders of Israel, and all the heads of the twelve tribes of Israel before him in Jerusalem, and they brought up the ark of the covenant that contained the tablets with the Ten Commandments written on them by God, the statutes, and the song of Moses out of the city of David, which is Zion. And all the elders of Israel came, and the priests took up the ark, and they brought the ark of the Lord, and the tabernacle of the congregation (which were nearly five hundred years old, from Moses's time), and all the holy vessels that were in the tabernacle (tent of meeting with God), and these did the priests, the Levites bring up.

> And the priests brought all these into the temple, into the most holy place [called the holy of holies, which only the high priest could enter once a year] under the wings of the cherubim for the cherubim spread forth their two wings over the ark, and the cherubim covered the ark. And it came to pass when the priests came out of the holy place, Solomon's temple [also called the first temple], that the cloud filled the house of the Lord.

And the priests could not stand to minister in the temple because the glory of the Lord had filled the house of the Lord. Once again God personally comes to inspect his new temple in the cloud (energy vehicle) built by King Solomon 487 years after inspecting his tabernacle (tent) in the cloud, which was built by Moses in the wilderness (Exod. 40:33). Two strikingly similar events happened nearly five hundred years apart. Another account is in (2 Chron. 5). After the Israelites praised God at the dedication of the temple, the cloud fills the temple.

Now let's turn to Elijah, who lived around 900 BC. Elijah told King Ahaziah of Israel (the country of Israel was now split into two kingdoms, Israel in the north, and Judah in the south) that he would die, and as Elijah was walking with Elisha, his disciple, he told Elisha that God was going to take him (Elijah).

And it came to pass as they walked and talked that a chariot of fire appeared (a similar description to the cloud and fire), and horses of fire, and parted them both asunder.

And Elijah went up by a whirlwind into the sky, into the chariot of fire, just as Moses went into the cloud and fire nearly five hundred years earlier.

Over nine hundred years later, Elijah was present with Moses talking to Jesus Christ before the three of them enter into God's energy vehicle in Luke 9:27, Matthew 10:1–9, and Mark 9:2–8.

In AD 32, Jesus took three of his disciples—Peter, John, and James—and went up a mountain to pray, and as he prayed, his countenance was altered, and his raiment was white and glistening. And Moses and Elijah (old friends who had spoken to Jesus centuries before), who appeared in glory (as resurrected beings), talked with Jesus of his coming death in Jerusalem. Peter told Jesus it was good for them all to be there witnessing those events, and while he spoke, a cloud came and overshadowed them.

Then Jesus, Moses, and Elijah went into the cloud. And a voice came out of the cloud, saying, "This is my son; listen to him." Can anything be clearer?

Then they saw Jesus alone; Moses and Elijah had gone in the cloud, and the cloud left at a fantastic speed, so it appeared to disappear.

These clouds are not rain clouds. Time and time again, it can be seen that these clouds, chariots of fire, fires at night, and so on contain beings that are not mortals.

CHAPTER 8

THE BOOK OF PSALMS

P salm 68, King David (Solomon's father): "Sing to God who rides upon the heavens, the chariots of God [clouds or energy vehicles] are twenty thousand, and thousands of angels. The Lord is among them as in Sinai [referring to God's interaction with the Israelites during the exodus from Egypt] as in the holy place."

"To him [God] that rides the heavens of heavens which were of old, God sends out his voice, a mighty voice." God's strength is in the clouds, which is a reference to these energy vehicles. Can anything be clearer? These clouds are not rain clouds. From Genesis to Revelation, these clouds and the beings in them interact with humanity and have immortal beings in them. These clouds had such an impact on the Israelites that they attributed God's strength to be in these clouds.

Psalm 97:1 says, "The Lord reigns, let the earth rejoice. Clouds and darkness are about him [not rain clouds]. A fire goes before him [energy]."

Psalm 99:1–9 says, "The Lord reigns. Moses and Aaron are among his priests, and Samuel among them who call his name, he spoke to them in the pillar of the cloud." Once again God or one of his angels spoke to Samuel from a cloud (energy vehicle).

Psalm 104 says, "Bless the Lord; thou art great; thou art clothed with majesty and honor, who covers thyself with light [energy] as with a garment, who makes the clouds [energy vehicles] his chariot." Can anything be plainer? These clouds are his chariot, or in modern terms, they are the way he chooses to travel.

Psalm 105:26–39 says, "He sent Moses his servant." Then the Psalm relates the plagues God visited on Egypt and pharaoh and the gods of Egypt. He (God) spread a cloud for a covering and fire to give light at night. This is the energy glowing at night. This is why the cloud appears to be different at night.

This is similar to Revelation 10:1, which says, "And I saw an angel come down from heaven clothed with a cloud." In other words, they do just that. These beings come from heaven in these clouds. To deny this is unbiblical and unchristian, for want of a better word.

The ancient Israelites sang songs about these energy beings in their energy vehicles. The beings travelled in these clouds, their chariots, and some human beings were privileged enough to enter inside them, including Moses, Elijah, and the being known to the world as Jesus Christ. Moses and Elijah came to visit Jesus Christ many centuries after their respective deaths, showing some of Jesus's disciples what the kingdom of God is—resurrection and immortality.

These beings appear to be made of energy. They're described as having the appearance of rainbows on their heads, faces that seem to radiate like the sun, and feet like pillars of fire. God is a sun in another description: Psalm 84:11.

Not made of solid matter as human beings are. We are made of atoms, molecules, tissues, organs, and so on. We're bound by the laws of physics, by gravity, by electromagnetic force, and other bonds.

Isaiah 19:1 says, "The burden of Egypt, behold the Lord rides upon a swift cloud and shall come into Egypt. And the idols of

Egypt shall be moved at his presence and the heart of Egypt shall be moved at his presence and the heart of Egypt shall melt." This time the prophet Isaiah, who lived around 750 BC, talked about a being (the Lord) in a swift vehicle, which they called a cloud.

CHAPTER 9
THE PROPHET EZEKIEL, 600 BC

E zekiel 1:1–28 says, "Now it came to pass in the thirtieth year, in the fourth month, in the fifth day of the month, as I was by the river Chebar [in modern-day Iraq] with the other captives [those captured by the Babylonians during the Babylonian captivity] the heavens opened, and I saw visions of God, and I looked and saw a whirlwind come out of the north. A great cloud and a fire enfolding itself, and a brightness was about it, and out of the midst the color of amber, out of the midst of the fire."

It then goes on to describe what looked like living creatures. "And the living creatures all went straight forward wherever the spirit went, they turned not where they went" (they didn't walk like humans do).

Not subject to gravity and using a different method of locomotion than earth-based life.

As for the living creatures, their appearance was like burning coals of fire and like the appearance of lamps. This description is similar to the description in Genesis with Abraham thirteen hundred years previously. "It went up and down among the living creatures, and the fire was bright, and out of the fire went forth lightning. And the living creatures ran and returned with the appearance of a flash of lightning." Ezekiel was bewildered by their lightning-like appearance and movements.

The cloud appeared now in Babylon (modern-day southern Iraq), and then Ezekiel was shown Jerusalem.

Then the glory of the Lord went up from the cherub and stood over the threshold of the house, and the court was full of the brightness of the Lord's glory.

And the cherubim were lifted up—this is the same living creature that I saw by the river Chebar (in modern-day Iraq).

Then the glory of the Lord departed off the threshold of the house.

And the glory of the Lord went up from the midst of the city and stood upon the mountain that is on the east side of the city. Once again, the cloud and the glory of the Lord visited God's house—the temple in Jerusalem—four hundred years after they came in the time of King Solomon.

Ezekiel 11:17 states, "Thus says the Lord, 'I will gather you from the peoples you are among and assemble you out of the countries you have been scattered to, and I will give you the land of Israel. And [people] shall know that I am the Lord when I shall scatter them among the nations, and disperse them in the countries.'" Ezekiel was being told about the Jewish Diaspora centuries before it happened in history.

Ezekiel 12:25 says, "For I am the Lord, I shall speak and the word that I speak shall come to pass." Declaring history before it happens.

> And I will bring you out from the people you are among, and gather you out of the countries where you are scattered with a mighty hand and a stretched out arm.
> And you shall know that I am the Lord God, when I shall bring you into the land of Israel, into the country which I gave your ancestors.

This message is from a being who visited the prophet Ezekiel twenty-six hundred years ago in a cloud. What happened? The Jews had scattered into many countries, and at the end of the World War II, they returned to the land of Israel after thousands of years. Coincidence? Or is this more likely? Ezekiel 12:25 says, "I am the Lord, I shall speak, and the word that I speak shall come to pass."

Not too hard to authenticate and confirm. A simple search on the Internet will quickly provide evidence. Type *Babylonian captivity of the Jews* and *Jewish Diaspora* on the Internet, and within twenty minutes you should have an understanding of these events.

Once again the mention of energy vehicles and energy beings in the forms of angels and clouds of the Lord.

CHAPTER 10

THE BOOK OF DANIEL, 550 BC

Daniel was a Jew taken captive by the Babylonians as a young man, who worked in the royal court of Babylonia, and later the Persians when they conquered the Babylonian Empire (known to us as Daniel in the lion's den in 550 BC). Daniel 2:1 says, "In the second year of the reign of Nebuchadnezzar 604 BC [Nebuchadnezzar ruled Babylonia from 605 BC to 562 BC.].

The king had a strange dream [or vision] which troubled him severely. He commanded his wise men and soothsayers to tell him what he dreamed [or saw in the vision] and what it meant. If they could not, he commanded that they be slain."

Daniel prayed to God and was given a vision of what the king saw and its meaning. Daniel came to the king and told him there was a God in heaven, a revealer of secrets, and he told the king what he had dreamed and what it meant.

The king was given a vision of world history up until the time when God will set up an eternal kingdom here on earth, one that will not be conquered, that will eliminate war, disease, suffering, and finally death itself. There will be a world empire with God at its head and Jesus Christ and his elect (or 144,002 chosen ones) under him (Dan. 2:44).

Daniel 7:1 says, "I saw in the night visions, and behold, one like the son of man came with the clouds of heaven." Once again, these clouds come from heaven. The Son of Man is a title for Jesus Christ. "And came to the Ancient of Days, and they brought him near before him." The Ancient of Days is a title for God the father, the creator.

Jesus travelled in these energy vehicles to God in the same way Jesus left the earth after his resurrection, and he will return (according to the Bible) in the same way and set up his worldwide kingdom, with Jerusalem as its capitol.

In Daniel 10:6, Daniel is beside a river, and a being approaches him. "His body was like the beryl, and his face as the appearance of lightning, and his eyes as lamps of fire, and his arms and his feet like in color to polished brass, and the voice of his words like the voice of a great multitude." This is a description of an energy being.

Then the energy being says to him, "Fear not, Daniel, for from the first day you humbled yourself before God your words were heard, and I have come because of your words" (Dan. 10:12).

The being tells Daniel that a mighty Greek king shall come and rule a vast realm, and after him, his kingdom shall break up into four parts. The king is Alexander the Great. This all happened two hundred years after Daniel.

The being told Daniel the course of world events. The last message he heard was that the words would be sealed up (not to be understood) till the end times and that knowledge would greatly increase, which it certainly has since Daniel's time.

And that "none of the wicked shall understand, but the wise shall understand." Do you understand this? The wicked cannot understand it; they are blocked from understanding.

To understand, you need to take the leap of faith and humble yourself before God, as Daniel did.

Then as the Bible describes, "The scales shall fall from your eyes and you will see reality." What is really happening in the world is what these beings have told the prophets. The ability to see through religious and atheistic deception and understand the signs of the times.

Daniel revealed that these clouds come to God with beings inside them, similar to the description in the book of Psalm 68:17.

"The chariots of God are twenty thousand, and who makes the clouds his chariot." Once again, clouds are energy vehicles and energy beings. Also the wicked (those who say God and the Bible are fairy tales) will not understand, but the wise (those who, like Daniel, humble themselves before God) will understand the scriptures. Which category are you in?

CHAPTER 11
THE BOOK OF NEHEMIAH, 440 BC

The Persian king Artaxerxes allowed Nehemiah to return to Jerusalem to help rebuild the temple that was destroyed by the Babylonians in 586 BC.

And the priests talked to the assembled Jews. "God saw our affliction in Egypt [in the time of Moses, one thousand years earlier] and showed signs and wonders upon pharaoh and all the people of Egypt." This passage refers to the plagues of Egypt and the judgment against Egypt's gods; Egypt's gods could do nothing to stop the plagues. And God divided the sea, which allowed the Israelites to walk through on dry land, and then he allowed the sea to collapse, killing the Egyptian army.

> Moreover you led the Israelites in the day by a cloudy pillar and in the night by a pillar of fire.

"You came down upon Mount Sinai and spoke with them from heaven [from the energy vehicle]." Can anything be plainer? The clouds came from heaven, or the sky. Led the Israelites in daytime in a cloudy pillar of energy and at night in a pillar of fire. Why the difference? The same as if you turn a light globe on in the daytime and then turn it on at night.

And [the Israelites] made the golden calf, and said, "This is the God that brought us up out of the land of Egypt."

"Yet you in your mercy helped them in the wilderness, the pillar of the cloud departed not from them by day, to show them the way, nor the pillar of fire by night, to give them light and the way they should go. Forty years you helped them in the wilderness." Once again, this happened in the time of Nehemiah, in 440 BC. One thousand years after Moses, the Jewish priests told the populace about God being in these clouds and fire and about how God helped the Israelites leave Egypt and survive in the desert.

Nehemiah 1:8 says, "Remember I beseech thee, the word that you commanded your servant Moses saying, 'I will scatter you abroad among the nations.'"

History attests to this happening: the Jews have been scattered among the nations.

Nehemiah 1:9 says, "But if you turn unto me, and keep my commandments, and do them, though you were cast out to the uttermost parts of heaven, yet will I gather you from there, and will bring you to the place where I have chosen to set my name." The place the author is referring to is Jerusalem.

This has happened with the founding of the state of Israel on May 14, 1948.

This ends the Old Testament record of the clouds of the Lord (including the chariots of the Lord, the pillar of fire, the whirlwind from heaven). My personal description is energy vehicle. The beings and clouds look like they are composed of or are covered with energy.

It would be easy to assume the clouds and chariots are spaceships from an alien world that have come to our planet, but finish reading about the clouds' relationship with us in the New Testament before you hold on to that assumption.

The technologies being described by the Bible writers are way past our current levels of development.

Parting the sea and holding it in place with no visible means of support are highly suggestive of a force field. It suggests the energy vehicles are in control of gravity, not subject to it.

The whirlwind that took Elijah up into the chariot of the Lord also suggests mastery over gravity, similar to the pillars from the cloud.

The descriptions also suggest superspeed within the earth's atmosphere, and the ability to suspend itself in the sky with no visible means.

The descriptions of the plagues of Egypt, which were also an attack on the Egyptian priests and their gods, also suggest mastery over the natural world (not described here but easily referenced in the Bible). It is highly likely these clouds were involved in other matters recorded in the Old Testament and some that were not recorded at all.

If, after reading and confirming what I have written so far in this book, you believe humanity is the highest level of intelligence to have been on this planet, I don't know what to say, except perhaps good luck. I also suggest you read the summary of the clouds of the Lord in the New Testament, which is even more astounding.

"I am God, and there is none like me, declaring the end from the beginning and from ancient times things not yet done" (Isa. 46). That's quite a statement. Is it true? Let's take a look.

Isaiah is believed to have lived in the eighth century BC. He is believed to have prophesied the birth and ministry of Jesus Christ. Let's start with one of his prophecies that is easily verifiable in history—Isaiah 44:28: "Cyrus is my shepherd, he shall perform my work, even saying to Jerusalem you shall be built, and the temple and its foundations shall be laid."

Isaiah 45 says, "Thus says the Lord to his [chosen servant], Cyrus, whose right hand I have held, to subdue [conquer] nations, and I the Lord will give you treasures, that you may know that I, the Lord, who calls you by name, am the Lord of Israel. For Jacob my servant's sake, and Israel my chosen, I have even called you by your name, even though you don't know me." When did Isaiah live?

Cyrus the Great (580–529 BC) was the first Persian emperor. He founded Persia by uniting the two original Iranian tribes—the Medes and the Persians. Although he was a great conqueror who at one point controlled one of the greatest empires ever seen, he is best remembered for his unprecedented tolerance and benevolent attitude toward those he defeated.

After his victory over the Medes, he started a government for his new kingdom, incorporating both Mede and Persian nobles as civil officials. After completing the conquest of Asia Minor, he led his armies to the eastern frontiers of his empire. Hyrcania and Parthia were already part of the Median kingdom. Further east, he conquered Drangiana, Arachosia, Margiana, and Bactria. After crossing the Oxus River, he reached the Jaxartes River, where he built fortified towns with the object of defending the farthest frontier of his kingdom against the nomadic tribes of central Asia.

The victories to the east led him again to the west and led him to attack Babylon and Egypt. When he conquered Babylon, he did so to cheers from the Jewish community, who welcomed him as a liberator. He allowed the Jews to return to the Promised Land after their captivity in Babylonia. He showed great respect toward the religious beliefs and cultural traditions of other races. These attributes earned him the respect and homage of all the people over whom he ruled.

Cyrus the Great, in his capital Pasargad, in modern-day Iran. The victory over Babylon expressed all the facets of the policy of conciliation that Cyrus had followed until then. He presented himself not as a conqueror but as a liberator and the legitimate successor to the crown. He also declared the first charter of human rights known to humanity (see Cyrus's stellar in the London Museum). Cyrus had the wisdom to leave the institutions of each kingdom he attached to the Persian crown unchanged. In 539 BC, he allowed more than forty thousand Jews to leave Babylon and return to Palestine, where they finished building the Jewish temple. This step was in line with his policy to bring peace to humanity and liberate nations from slavery.

Cyrus was upright, a great leader of men, generous, and benevolent. The Hellenes, whom he conquered, regarded him as Lawgiver, and the Jews called him the Anointed of the Lord (as Isaiah's prophecy stated).

Isaiah is recognized by scholars as being alive in the eighth century BC, and Cyrus lived over one hundred years later in the sixth century BC. So if Isaiah were alive in the eighth century BC, then Isaiah prophesied that Cyrus would rule the largest empire in the world at that time over one hundred years before he was born.

Is this definite proof of the existence of God? No, there are alternative explanations. Isaiah might have lived at the same time as Cyrus, or perhaps Cyrus's parents heard about the prophesy and named their child Cyrus to help him gain power. So did Cyrus come to prominence because God declared it, or did he do so by natural means? Cyrus is just one of many prophecies that God declared (I am God, declaring things from ancient times). So let's investigate the other prophecies.

The prophecy of the Passover being kept and passed down through the ages.

The Israelites left slavery in Egypt after God won the contests against Egypt's so-called gods; the last contest ended in the deaths of the Egyptians' firstborn sons—an event that is still celebrated today as the Passover by the Jews and some Christian churches. The destroyer passed over the houses of the Israelites and only killed the Egyptians.

Exodus 12:12–14 says, "This day you shall keep as a memorial, you shall keep this feast to the Lord throughout your generations, you shall keep it as a feast forever, when your children ask you what is the meaning of this feast you shall say, 'It is the Lord's Passover,' who passed over the houses of the children of Israel in Egypt when he killed the Egyptians."

Thirty-five hundred years later, the Passover is still being told and celebrated.

The Israelites left Egypt after being there for 430 years.

So here once again, God's prophecy is 100 percent true—the Passover is still celebrated.

Deuteronomy 28:15 says, "But it shall come to pass if you will not listen to God and not do his commandments, then all these curses will come upon you and overtake you."

Deuteronomy 28:25 says, "God shall cause you to be smitten by your enemies, and you will be removed into all the [countries] of the earth." Historians refer to this event as the great Jewish Diaspora, but the Jews only account for two Israeli tribes and are known because they have kept their identity for all this time; the other ten tribes are referred to in history as the ten lost tribes of Israel.

Deuteronomy 28:37 says, "And you shall become an astonishment, a proverb and a byword among all the nations where God shall lead you." Antisemitism is hatred of the Jews, which has happened throughout history and is still with us today.

Deuteronomy 28:64–66 says, "And God shall scatter you among all people, from one end of the earth to the other. And among these nations you shall find no ease. And your life shall hang in doubt before you."

This is exactly what has happened in history. The Jews have been persecuted and feared for their lives throughout the world. After the Nazi Holocaust of World War II, the Jews finally returned to Israel and set up their own state in 1948 to be able to determine their own fate. So far this is the third indisputable prophecy to have come to pass. Don't worry; this is only the start of many prophecies that have come to pass. Only fools say none of God's prophecies have come to pass.

So what is the real message of the Bible? Is it that some people will go to some vague heaven for being good, and the others will go to some terrible hell, where they will suffer unbelievable pain and suffering for all eternity? Is that what you believe? The real story is quite surprising, but the Bible states that God himself will come to planet Earth to live with his children one thousand years after Jesus Christ returns in the clouds of the Lord and sets up his government for all of us, except for the incorrigibly wicked, who will not leave their evil ways.

This is made clear by God's statement that he doesn't want to lose even one of us, and after the final judgment, the entire universe will be placed under our custody, similar to the earth being currently under humanity's dominion. This is why God refers to himself as being our father, and Jesus Christ refers to himself as our brother, who loves us enough to suffer extreme agony and death to show us the way to immortality. Ultimately there are two ways with two differing ends: one is God's way, which leads to eternal life with God and Jesus as our father and older brother; the other way leads to eternal death. The Bible describes the dead being resurrected to life. Initially, 144,002 at the return of Christ, and one thousand years later, all the other people who have ever lived. It all makes so much sense once it is properly understood. Don't be fooled; investigate eternal wonderful life without suffering or eternal death with no suffering (euthanasia) for yourself— these are the real choices and the only choices.

What will happen over the next twenty-five years? The being who is referred to as Jesus Christ left a record of the events leading up to his return in the clouds of the Lord. Such events are recorded in the Olivet Prophecy. Make no mistake: Bible prophecy has always been fulfilled and always will be. Do not be fooled by those who do not understand prophecy; the clouds of the Lord is one area of understanding that can truly open one's mind to the real truth.

John 20:30 says, "But these are written, so you might believe that Jesus is the son of God." In other words, prophecy. You can believe Christ was an immortal because he revealed the future.

When you understand prophecy, you understand Jesus was no ordinary mortal. You understand the future before it happens, and your faith is not blind; it is extremely informed. Matthew 24:34 says, "Verily I say unto you, this generation will not pass, till all these things be fulfilled." Luke 21:32 says, "Verily I say unto you, this generation shall not pass away till all be fulfilled." Which generation are these verses talking about?

Many atheists claim Jesus was talking about his generation, but Jesus clearly stated that "the Gospel must be preached to the entire world, then the end of this age will come." Only in this generation is that being fulfilled. The Gospel (meaning good news) is finally being preached to the whole world with the use of the Internet and satellite TV.

Other prophecies from Deuteronomy to Revelation state the Jews and other Israelites would be dispersed throughout the entire world and then brought back to Israel in the last days.

This happened with the establishment of the nation of Israel in 1948, after the Nazi Holocaust. Other prophecies say that Christ will come back in the last days, just before humanity destroys everything.

This only became possible in the 1950s when the United States and the Soviet Union built up nuclear arsenals capable of killing everyone. How did they know all this would occur within one generation?

Quite simply, the message was from the creator, God.

In the Bible, God states, "I am God, and there is none like me, declaring from ancient times things that will come to pass." Did these things come to pass? They have, and more are coming.

Many leading atheists claim nothing the Bible states as prophecy has come to pass, and when some points are shown, such as the Jews returning to Israel, they claim they are self-fulfilled (i.e., the Jews made them happen). The information on the next page will show you how ridiculous this statement is; once you study the Bible extensively and humbly, you can see the arrogant, self-inflated atheist views are extremely stupid and simplistic, just as the Bible prophesied they would be. Second Peter 3 says, "Knowing this first, that there shall come in the last days scoffers, walking after their own lusts [perverted, unnatural sexual behaviors, such as porn and related filth], and saying, 'Where is the promise of his coming?' For since the fathers fell asleep, all things continue as they were from the beginning of the creation." It is easy to see that many reject God and the Bible for their own moral reasons, not logical ones, and others are merely indoctrinated into atheistic or falsely religious views.

There is one word you will hear from atheists, whether they have little education or they are Oxford or Harvard "trained" (brainwashed) educators. That word is *coincidence*, and it's used over and over again to explain extreme levels of design.

One that comes to mind is the moon, which appears to be about the same size as the sun in the sky, even though the moon is tiny in comparison. The reason for this is that it is at a relative distance to the earth. It is also at just the right distance to allow human life to exist on the earth.

I remember an atheist scientist saying that "owing to an amazing coincidence," the moon, even though it is four hundred times smaller than the sun, is four hundred times closer to the earth, and that is the reason the sun and moon appear to be the same size in our sky. Is this an amazing coincidence, or is this more likely?

Genesis 16 says, "And God made two great lights, the greater light [the sun] to rule the day, and the lesser light to rule the night [the moon]."

Beings able to travel from someplace that is perhaps billions of light-years away or maybe not even in our universe would certainly be able to move the moon into a desired orbit around the earth. We launch satellites and place them into our desired orbits around the planet, and we haven't even walked on Mars yet.

Beings also tell us about a war starting in Iraq. The Iraq War has unleashed massive hostility toward the West, unbalanced the balance of power in that entire region, and unleashed Islamic ji-had, with Shi'ite and Sunni jihadists unleashing campaigns of ter-ror bombings on each other and the rest of the world.

A war that will ultimately kill one-third of humanity—in other words, a world war surpassing the world wars we have seen so far. In World War I, nine million people died, and in World War II, seventy million people died. How many will World War III kill? One-third of the earth's population.

It has already started. At the end of the World War II, US Army General Douglas Macarthur (1880–1964) stated, "We have had our last chance, war has become so destructive, so dreadful, if we do not find an alternative, we will destroy civilization."

Macarthur was at that time in charge of the Allied occupa-tion of Japan after their surrender to the Allies, which only came about after the United States detonated nuclear bombs over the Japanese cities of Hiroshima and Nagasaki, totally destroying them. The United States threatened to destroy the rest of Japan with more nukes because of the suicidal and homicidal fanaticism of the Japanese. Today is no different; we have fanatics who launch suicidal attacks across the planet. What will happen when these fanatics get weapons of mass destruction?

After the World War I, the League of Nations was formed to prevent another world war. They utterly failed with the World War II twenty years later, which caused about ten times more destruction.

The United Nations, the successor to the League of Nations, has not been able to prevent or stop many small wars in Rwanda, Congo, Sierra Leone, and dozens of other places, and the United Nations is not stopping World War III.

When Albert Einstein died on April 18, 1955, he left a piece of writing ending in an unfinished sentence—a warning. These were his last words:

> In essence, the conflict that exists today is no more than an old-style struggle for power, once again presented to humanity in semireligious trappings. The difference is that, this time, the development of <u>atomic power</u> has imbued the struggle with a ghostly character; for both parties know and admit that, should the quarrel deteriorate into actual war, <u>humanity is doomed</u>.

Despite this knowledge, statesmen in responsible positions on both sides of the conflict continue to employ the well-known technique of seeking to intimidate and demoralize the opponent by marshaling superior military strength. They do so even though such a policy entails the risk of war and doom. Not one statesman in a position of responsibility has dared to pursue the only course that holds out any promise of peace—the course of supranational security—since for a statesman to follow such a course would be tantamount to political suicide. Political passions, once they have been fanned into flame, exact their victims.

Here we have warnings from two of the most influential men of the preceding generation about our future; even without the prophecies of the Bible, it is plain to see the human race is headed for real trouble. With an accurate knowledge of the Bible's prophecies, it is possible to understand what is going to happen years before it actually happens. With an inaccurate understanding of the prophecies, obviously an inaccurate understanding of events will occur. This has been happening for centuries, and it ultimately will still occur till Christ returns in the clouds of the Lord.

We have enough weapons of mass destruction today to destroy all life, and many more countries will obtain these weapons of mass destruction over the next decade. Following the pattern of the previous world wars, the death rate is likely to be much higher.

Unless someone or something intervenes, it would likely be much higher than World War I or World War II, perhaps even complete genocide. We need a savior; let's hope one will come in the clouds of the Lord.

CHAPTER 12
WHAT DID THESE BEINGS SAY? DID IT OCCUR?

Did these beings (angels) relay anything of importance? Are their revelations backed up by history or science?

Let's have a look at some of the plain and simple revelations and see whether they occurred independently from the Bible or other religious sources.

The Bible says in Isaiah 46:9, "Remember the former things of old: For I am God, and there is none else, I am God and there is none like me." Isaiah 46:10 says, "Declaring the end from the beginning, and from ancient times the things that are not yet done," saying "my counsel shall stand, and I will do all my pleasure." In other words, whatever God declares will happen, regardless of what anyone says or thinks. Even if something was prophesied by God in ancient times, it will come to pass. Has it?

Most people are aware of the Jews forming the modern-day state of Israel after the Holocaust in World War II in 1948. Did they say anything about that?

Deuteronomy 28:1 says, "And it will happen, if you will listen to God and obey all his commandments. Which I command you this day, that God will set you high above all nations of the world."

Moses told the Israelites in the desert what God had stated—that if they obeyed him, they would be the world's leading nation and that everything would go well for them.

Deuteronomy 28:15 says, "But it shall come to pass if you will not listen to God and not do his commandments, then all these curses will come upon you and overtake you."

Deuteronomy 28:25 says, "God shall cause you to be smitten by your enemies, and you will be removed into all the kingdoms [countries] of the earth."

That is history; the Israelites even burnt their children as sacrifices to Baal (a pagan deity). The great Jewish Diaspora, when the Israelites were removed to other nations throughout the world. But the Jews are only made up of two tribes of the Israelites and are known because they have kept their identity for all this time. (Napoleon commented on how the Jews kept their identity with such tenacity.) The other ten tribes are referred to in history as the ten lost tribes of Israel.

Deuteronomy 28:37 says, "And you shall become an astonishment, a proverb and a byword among all the nations where God shall lead you." Antisemitism is hatred of the Jews, which has happened throughout history and is still with us today.

Deuteronomy 28:64–66 says, "And God shall scatter you among all people, from one end of the earth to the other. And among these nations you shall find no ease. And your life shall hang in doubt before you."

This is exactly what has happened in history. The Jews have been persecuted and feared for their lives throughout the world throughout history. After the Nazi Holocaust of World War II, the Jews finally returned to Israel and set up their own state in 1948 to be able to determine their own fate without being persecuted. Deuteronomy 30;1 says,

> And it shall come to pass when all these things have come upon you, the blessing and the curse, which I have set before you and you shall remember them in all the nations God has driven you to.
> And return to the Lord, your God, and you obey him again according to all that I command you this day, you and your children, with all your heart and all your soul.
> Then the Lord your God will turn your captivity, and have compassion on you, and will return and gather you from all the nations, where the Lord your God has scattered you. If any of you has been driven out to the outermost part of the earth the Lord God will gather you from there, and will bring you back into this land, which your fathers' possessed, and you shall possess it and he will do you good and multiply you more than your fathers.

This is exactly what has happened: a homeless, wandering group of tribes formed an ancient nation, turned against God, and ultimately lost their nation and were dispersed throughout the world. And then after turning back to God during and after the Holocaust of World War II, they formed the modern nation of Israel.

Atheists say the Jews returned because they knew about the prophecy that they would return, or some even say that the Jews of today are not related to the Jews of the times of the ancient Israelites. The deception in the world is profound; people even believe the Jews murder Catholic children for their blood to make their Passover bread.

Would the Jews intentionally spread to all parts of the world and be hated (antisemitism), killed, tortured, persecuted, executed, and so on? No, that is a ridiculous assumption put forward by militant atheists and religious fanatics to deny God or justify murdering the Jews. And there is much more.

Deuteronomy 31:15–19 says, "I have set before you this day life and good, and death and evil...I call heaven and earth to record this day against you, that I have set before you life and death, blessing and cursing, therefore choose life, that you and your descendants may live."

The Jews have been persecuted throughout history, as was foretold in the Bible. The Assyrians conquered and deported the northern ten tribes of Israel to the land of the Medes in modern-day Iran, and the Babylonians conquered the southern two tribes (the Jews) and took them to Babylon (modern-day Iraq). The Romans enslaved the Jews and ultimately banned them from Jerusalem on pain of death in AD 136. Huge numbers of Jews were killed and taken to Rome as slaves.

The Roman Catholic Church persecuted the Jews throughout the ages, stating that the Jews were the murderers of Christ, with popes issuing decrees against Jews and inciting hatred.

The Greek Orthodox Church also instigated pogroms against the Jews, with many, many being tortured and killed. Islam has also killed and persecuted the Jews throughout the ages, and now in modern times, they have exiled them from many Islamic nations and regularly attack them, swearing to annihilate them and finish off Hitler's final solution to the Jewish problem. The grand mufti of Jerusalem issued a fatwa against the Jews in the 1920s, and he became Hitler's ally in 1939.

Communist Russia imprisoned the Jews and persecuted them (eventually allowing thousands to migrate to Israel in the 1980s). Even this tiny amount of information should show you the accuracy of this unlikely prophecy. Keep a humble and open mind, and prove all things; don't believe all things that you are told to believe or that you want to believe.

Carefully read the prophecies (the Jews being an astonishment, a proverb, and a byword—*antisemitism*), the Jews' lives hanging in the balance, and the Israelites being dispersed throughout the world and being brought back to the ancient land of Israel.

CHAPTER 13
PERSECUTION OF THE JEWS

- 135 BC: The Syrian Greek king Antiochus Epiphanes desecrated the second Jewish temple, which was built by the remnant of Jews who had returned from Babylonian and Persian captivity, causing the Hasmonaean Revolt against the Greek authorities.
- AD 70: Titus of Rome took Jerusalem and killed one million Jews, as was prophesied by Jesus. (See Jesus wept.)
- AD 136: There was a third Jewish revolt. The Jews were killed and banned from living in Jerusalem under pain of death. (The Romans renamed Jerusalem Aelia Capitolina.)
- AD 306: The catholic council in Spain banned Christians and Jews from marrying each other.
- AD 1012: Emperor Henry of Germany expelled the Jews from Mainz, beginning German persecution over nine hundred years before Hitler.
- AD 1096: The first crusade started, and crusaders massacre Jews in the Rhineland.
- AD 1144: The first recorded case of Jewish blood libel happened, where anti-Jewish elements claim the Jews used Christian children's blood for their Passover bread (God

commanded that Passover be observed down through the ages but obviously without killing children), slitting a child's throat and draining his or her blood to make the bread. (The Islamic propaganda machine is claiming now that this is real, with millions of Muslims believing it today.)

- AD 1190: There was a massacre of Jews in England.
- AD 1290: The Jews were exiled from England.
- AD 1298: Jews were murdered in Germany.
- AD 1306: Jews were exiled from France.
- AD 1348: Jews were blamed for the black death (also known as the bubonic plague). The Jews did not suffer as much from the plague because they followed the instructions from God in Leviticus concerning cleanliness, disease, and isolating the sick from the population, causing the Catholic and Orthodox hierarchy to accuse them of being in league with the devil.
- AD 1389: There were massacres in Bohemia, Spain.
- AD 1421: Hundreds of Jews were burned at the stake by the authorities of the Catholic Inquisition. (France had already burnt many Jews at the stake by this time.)
- AD 1480: More Jews burnt at the stake in Spain.
- AD 1483: Jews were exiled from Poland, Lithuania, Sicily, and Portugal.
- AD 1492: All the Jews were exiled from Spain by Queen Isabella and King Ferdinand.
- AD 1510: Jews were exiled from Brandenburg, Germany.
- AD 1569: Jews were exiled from the papal states by the pope.
- AD 1593: Jews were exiled from Bavaria and Italy.
- AD 1598: Jews were executed for blood libel—accused of killing Christian children for Passover bread—and were executed by being quartered, or ripped into quarters.
- AD 1648: One hundred thousand Jews were killed in Ukraine by the Cossacks.

- AD 1715: Pope Pius VI ordered an edict against the Jews.
- AD 1768: Twenty thousand Jews were massacred in Poland.
- AD 1805: Jews were massacred in Algeria (so much for peaceful Muslims).
- AD 1840: Jews were again accused of blood libel in Damascus, Syria.
- AD 1853: Jews were accused of blood libel by the Orthodox Church in Russia.
- AD 1881: One hundred thousand Jews were killed or raped in pogroms in Kiev, Ukraine.
- AD 1919: Three thousand Jews were killed in Hungarian pogroms.
- AD 1929: Muslims massacred hundreds of Jews in Hebron, cutting the heads off Jewish children and stabbing their mothers to death. (See British police chief Ray Cafferata's testimony to the British court.)
- AD 1939–1945: Millions of Jews were massacred in death camps by the Nazis.
- AD 1948: Jews were murdered and exiled across the Muslim world.
- AD 1948 to the present: There have been many, many attacks by Muslims against Israel and Jews across the world, with Muslims swearing to slaughter the Jews and drink the blood of the Jews.

Deuteronomy 28:15 says, "If you do not follow my commandments you will be cursed."

In Zechariah 12:2, God says he will make Jerusalem a "cup of trembling to the people round about it and the nations surrounding it shall lay siege against it," which is precisely what is happening today.

The Islamic countries surrounding Jerusalem and Israel are involved in planning its destruction and its people's conversion to Islam. The Bible describes what is currently happening in the book of Psalms, which was written in King David's time, three thousand years ago. Psalm 83:3 says that the Islamic countries of Egypt, Iran, Iraq, Lebanon, Jordan, and Turkey "have taken crafty counsel against [Israel]." Psalm 83:4 says that the Islamic countries "have said, come and let us stop them [the Israelis] from becoming a nation, that the nation of Israel will be no more." And Psalm 83:5 says, "For they [the Islamic countries] have consulted together with one mind, they are working together against Israel." This is exactly what has been happening since the Jews returned to Israel in 1948 and even before that. The Muslim Brotherhood in Egypt (a worldwide Sunni Islamist organization), with its offspring Hamas in Gaza, which has constantly been attacking Israel, the Shi'ite mullahs of Iran with their Shi'ite offspring Hezbollah in Lebanon (responsible for killing hundreds of US soldiers in Lebanon and having a war against Israel) have all sworn to destroy the Jewish state of Israel, and they call it a cancer that must be destroyed, just as God prophesied in the Bible three thousand years ago.

When you have a proper understanding of the Bible, you start to get an understanding of what is going to happen because as the Bible says, God declares what is going to happen from ancient times, and he has the power to either know it is going to happen or has the ability to make it happen. The history of humanity has been prerecorded to some extent to show those willing to follow God what will happen, and you can be sure that whatever God declares will happen, regardless of whatever any human being says.

Jeremiah 30:1 (in 600 BC) says, "The word that came to Jeremiah from the Lord, saying, 'Thus speaks the Lord of Israel, saying, "Write what I have told you in a book."'" Much the same as Moses had to write in a book, the apostle John was also commanded to write in a book.

"For the days are coming when I will bring Israel and Judah into captivity, fear not I will save you from afar, from the land of their captivity."

"And Jacob [the Jews] shall return, though I will make an end of all nations where I scatter you, I will not make a full end of you." All the empires have passed into history—the Assyrians, the Babylonians, the Persians, the Greeks, the Romans, the Ottomans, and the Nazis—but the Jews have been preserved; this is unbelievable but true.

"But I will correct you in measure and will not leave you unpunished." The Jews have certainly been punished. "Therefore all those that devour you shall be devoured"; once again the nations that devoured the Jews have themselves been devoured by other nations. Jeremiah 33:7 says, "I will cause the captive Jews to return and the captive Israelites." The Jews have returned to Israel, but the other Israelites have not yet. Jeremiah 34:17 says, "I will make you to be removed to all the kingdoms of the earth." Did this happen? Very much so.

"Again I will build you and you will be built. You shall plant vines in Samaria [the West Bank]. Behold I will bring them from the north country [Europe] and gather them from the coasts of the earth, hear the word of the Lord O nations he that scattered Israel shall gather him. They shall come and sing in Zion [Jerusalem], then the virgin shall dance." Look at the videos of the young women dancing at the declaration of Israel in 1948.

God said Babylon would be destroyed and not be rebuilt; has it? Jerusalem and many other cities are still with us, but there aren't any international flights to Babylon International Airport, are there? Why? Because God decreed it thousands of years ago.

CHAPTER 14
ARCHAEOLOGY

A rchaeological findings contradict the contentions of biblical minimalists and other revisionists. There are many more, however, that corroborate biblical evidence, and the following list provides only the most significant discoveries.

A Common Flood Story
Not only the Hebrews (Gen. 6–8) but also the Mesopotamians, Egyptians, and Greeks all report a flood in primordial times. A list of Sumerian kings from circa 2100 BC divides itself into two categories: those kings who ruled before a great flood and those who ruled after it. One of the earliest examples of Sumero-Akkadian literature, *The Gilgamesh Epic*, describes a great flood sent as punishment by the gods, with humanity saved only when the pious Utnapishtim (a.k.a. the Mesopotamian Noah) built a ship and saved the animal world by loading them onto it. A later Greek counterpart, the story of Deucalion and Pyrrha, tells of a couple who survived a great flood sent by an angry Zeus. Taking refuge atop Mount Parnassus (a.k.a. the Greek Ararat), they supposedly repopulated the earth by heaving stones behind them that sprang into human beings.

The Code of Hammurabi

The Code of Hammurabi is a seven-foot black diorite stela that was discovered at Susa and is presently located in the Louvre Museum. It contains 282 engraved laws of the Babylonian king Hammurabi (1750 BC). The common basis for this law code is the *lex talionis* (the law of the tooth), showing that there was a common Semitic law of retribution in the ancient Near East that is clearly reflected in the Pentateuch. Exodus 21:23–25, for example, reads: "But if there is serious injury, you are to take life for life, eye for eye, tooth for tooth, hand for hand, foot for foot."

The Nuzi Tablets

Some twenty thousand cuneiform clay tablets were discovered at the ruins of Nuzi, east of the Tigris River. They are datable to circa 1500 BC, and they reveal institutions, practices, and customs that are remarkably congruent to those found in Genesis. These tablets include treaties, marriage arrangements, rules regarding inheritance and adoption, and the like.

The Existence of the Hittites

Genesis 23 reports that Abraham buried Sarah in the Cave of Machpelah, which he purchased from Ephron the Hittite. Second Samuel 11 tells of David's adultery with Bathsheba, the wife of Uriah the Hittite. A century ago, the Hittites were unknown outside of the Old Testament, and critics claimed that they were a figment of biblical imagination. In 1906, however, archaeologists digging east of Ankara, Turkey, discovered the ruins of Hattusas, the ancient Hittite capital at what is today called Boghazkoy, as well as its vast collection of Hittite historical records, which show an empire that was flourishing in the mid–second millennium BC. This critical challenge, among many others, was immediately proved worthless—a pattern that would often be repeated in the decades to come.

The Merneptah Stela

The Merneptah stela is a seven-foot slab engraved with hieroglyphics. It's also called the Israel stela, and it boasts of the Egyptian pharaoh's conquest of the Libyans and the people in Palestine, including the Israelites: "Israel—his seed is not." This is the earliest reference to Israel in nonbiblical sources and demonstrates that as of circa 1230 BC, the Hebrews were already living in the Promised Land.

Biblical Cities Attested Archaeologically

In addition to Jericho, places such as Haran, Hazor, Dan, Megiddo, Shechem, Samaria, Shiloh, Gezer, Gibeah, Beth Shemesh, Beth Shean, Beersheba, Lachish, and many other urban sites have been excavated, quite apart from larger and more obvious locations such as Jerusalem or Babylon. Such geographical markers are extremely significant in demonstrating that fact, not fantasy, is intended in the Old Testament historical narratives; otherwise, the specificity regarding these urban sites would have been replaced by once-upon-a-time narratives with only hazy geographical parameters, if any.

Israel's enemies in the Hebrew Bible likewise are not contrived but are solidly historical. Among the most dangerous of these were the Philistines, the people after whom Palestine itself would be named. Their earliest depiction is on the temple of Rameses III at Thebes, from circa 1150 BC, as people of the sea who invaded the delta area and later the coastal plain of Canaan. The pentapolis (five cities) they established—namely Ashkelon, Ashdod, Gaza, Gath, and Ekron—have all been excavated, at least in part, and some remain cities to this day. Such precise urban evidence measures favorably when compared with the geographical sites claimed in the holy books of other religious systems, which often have no basis whatever in reality.

Shishak's Invasion of Judah

First Kings 14 and 2 Chronicles 12 tell of Pharaoh Shishak's conquest of Judah in the fifth year of the reign of King Rehoboam, the brainless son of Solomon, and how Solomon's temple in Jerusalem was robbed of its treasures on that occasion. Shishak's victory is also commemorated in hieroglyphic wall carvings on the Temple of Amon at Thebes.

The Moabite Stone

Second Kings 3 reports that Mesha, the king of Moab, rebelled against the king of Israel following the death of Ahab. A three-foot stone slab, called the Mesha Stela, confirms the revolt by claiming triumph over Ahab's family in circa 850 BC, and it says that Israel perished forever.

Obelisk of Shalmaneser III

In 2 Kings 9–10, Jehu is mentioned as king of Israel (841–814 BC). That the growing power of Assyria was already encroaching on the northern kings prior to their ultimate conquest in 722 BC is demonstrated by a six-and-a-half-foot-tall black obelisk discovered in the ruins of the palace at Nimrud in 1846. On it, Jehu is shown kneeling before Shalmaneser III and offering tribute to the Assyrian king, the only relief we have to date of a Hebrew monarch.

Burial Plaque of King Uzziah

Down in Judah, King Uzziah ruled from 792 to 740 BC; he was a contemporary of Amos, Hosea, and Isaiah. Like Solomon, he began well and ended badly. In 2 Chronicles 26, his sin is recorded, which resulted in his being struck with leprosy later in life. When Uzziah died, he was interred in a "field of burial that belonged to the kings." His stone burial plaque has been discovered on the Mount of Olives, and it reads: "Here, the bones of Uzziah, King of Judah, were brought. Do not open."

Hezekiah's Siloam Tunnel Inscription

King Hezekiah of Judah ruled from 721 to 686 BC. Fearing a siege by the Assyrian king Sennacherib, Hezekiah preserved Jerusalem's water supply by cutting a tunnel through 1,750 feet of solid rock from the Gihon Spring to the Pool of Siloam inside the city walls (2 Kings 20; 2 Chron. 32). At the Siloam end of the tunnel, an inscription, which is presently in an archaeological museum in Istanbul, Turkey, celebrates this remarkable accomplishment. The tunnel is probably the only biblical site that has not changed its appearance in twenty-seven hundred years.

The Sennacherib Prism

After having conquered the ten northern tribes of Israel, the Assyrians moved southward to do the same to Judah (2 Kings 18–19). The prophet Isaiah, however, told Hezekiah that God would protect Judah and Jerusalem against Sennacherib (2 Chron. 32; Isa. 36–37). Assyrian records virtually confirm this. The cuneiform on a hexagonal, fifteen-inch baked clay prism found at the Assyrian capital of Nineveh describes Sennacherib's invasion of Judah in 701 BC. It claims that the Assyrian king shut Hezekiah inside Jerusalem "like a caged bird." Like the biblical record, however, it does not state that Sennacherib conquered Jerusalem, which the prism certainly would have done had this been the case. The Assyrians, in fact, bypassed Jerusalem on their way to Egypt, and the city did not fall until the time of Nebuchadnezzar and the neo-Babylonians in 586 BC. Sennacherib himself returned to Nineveh, where his own sons murdered him.

The Cylinder of Cyrus the Great

Second Chronicles 36:23 and Ezra 1 report that Cyrus the Great of Persia, after conquering Babylon, permitted Jews in Babylonia to return to their homeland. Isaiah had even prophesied this (Isa. 44:28). This tolerant policy of the founder of the Persian Empire is borne out by the discovery of a nine-inch clay cylinder found at Babylon from the time of its conquest, 539 BC, which reports Cyrus's victory and his subsequent policy of permitting Babylonian captives to return to their homes and even rebuild their temples.

So it goes. This list of correlations between Old Testament texts and the hard evidence of Near Eastern archaeology could easily be tripled in length. When it comes to the intertestamental and New Testament eras, as we might expect, the needle on the gauge of positive correlations simply goes off the scale.

To use terms such as *false testament* for the Hebrew Bible and to vaporize its earlier personalities into nonexistence have no justification whatever in terms of the mass of geographical, archaeological, and historical evidence that correlates so admirably with the scripture.

This, however, is quite typical of the way biblical matters are reported in today's news media. An extraordinary archaeological discovery that confirms the biblical record barely receives any notice in the press; this happened in November 1990 when the bones of a biblical personality were discovered for the first time. Generally, only one in a hundred knows that the remains of Joseph Caiaphas, the high priest who indicted Jesus before Pontius Pilate on Good Friday, were found at that time in an ossuary in the Peace Forest of Jerusalem, south of the temple area.

CHAPTER 15

NEW TESTAMENT

The New Testament, which confirms and continues on from the Old Testament, primarily describes the events from just before the birth of Jesus Christ, through his ministry, death (by crucifixion), and alleged resurrection three days later to the early days of the seven churches and through history to the present time and into the future.

The continuity of the involvement of the clouds of the Lord in the New Testament is absolutely astounding. Jesus Christ came with clouds. What are these clouds?

The ancient writers of the books of the Bible, all of whom claim they had contact with God through angels or visions in many different time periods, have inadvertently revealed interactions with beings and (for want of a better word) vehicles far superior to anything in our world's current level of technology.

The Israelites' descriptions were limited by their own scope of learning, and they called these vehicles clouds of the Lord, chariots of fire, and lights from heaven.

Inadvertently revealing vehicles of extreme levels of technology, which is to be expected of beings who are able to visit the earth from anywhere else in this universe, owing to the extreme distances and hazards of such a journey from outer space or from another dimension.

The Israelites' description of events past, present, and future fits into a pattern of logic that is well beyond the many writers from many different ancient time periods to collude on and falsify.

So much so that any rational, logical, thinking person today with any reasonable amount of intelligence would have to concede the Bible is based on facts. In other words, if you are intelligent enough to read this page and understand what is written on this page, you have enough intelligence to understand the rest of this book. You don't have to be a university professor at Oxford or Harvard. You only need to slightly open your mind and to have a tiny amount of humility.

What is the purpose of these beings who visit our planet in these clouds and chariots? According to these ancient writers (the Israelites), the answer will impact every human being who has ever lived. Read on, and make up your own mind.

The first mention of one of these incredible vehicles describes it as a star in the book of Matthew 2:1–9. Matthew describes it from the revelation of the three wise men from the east who are looking for the messiah (Jesus Christ).

The object the wise men were talking about appeared to look like a star (known now as the star of Bethlehem to the world) because it was high up in the earth's atmosphere, as opposed to witnesses in other parts of the Bible, who describe it looking like a cloud or a fire or a chariot of fire because it was closer to the observer. In the book of Revelation 10:1, John reported seeing an angel "clothed with a cloud" coming down to the earth in a vision given to him from Jesus Christ many years after Jesus's crucifixion.

The ancient Israelites followed a cloud for forty years in Moses's time. Moses went into a cloud and got the Ten Commandments from God (Exod. 24:15–18).The Bible reports an angel of the Lord coming to shepherds at night and the glory of the Lord shining around them (Luke 2:8–20). They were obviously terrified, and the angel responded to their terror, saying "fear not" and stating that the prophesied Messiah had been born (Jesus Christ).

The angel's vehicle looked like a star to these men, much like a helicopter or plane at night high up in the sky would appear to primitive men in today's world. It's quite easy to temporarily mistake a helicopter or plane for a star today.

Matthew 2:1 says, "Now when Jesus was born in Bethlehem, in King Herod's day, wise men from the east came to Jerusalem asking, 'Where is he that is born king of the Jews? For we have seen his star in the east and have come to worship him.'" King Herod was troubled upon hearing this (he feared for his kingship since he wasn't a Jew), and he asked the Jewish priests where Christ would be born. They replied he would be born in Bethlehem because it was written in the books of the prophets. Then Herod called the wise men and asked them when the star appeared, and he sent the wise men to Bethlehem to find the child for him, telling them he also wanted to worship the child. But he was planning to murder the child, thinking he was a danger to his rule.

The wise men left King Herod, and the star appeared. They followed it to Bethlehem, and it stopped above where the child was. Obviously, this was not a star like our sun. Similarly, Moses and the Israelites fourteen hundred years previously had followed a cloud by day and a fire by night. (The energy vehicle had been closer to the ground.)

The wise men rejoiced with "exceeding great joy." They went in to see the child and present gifts to the family, and then they left and returned to their homeland in the east without telling King Herod where the child was.

King Herod found out and responded by slaughtering the children under the age of two in the area, an event that was also prophesied in the Old Testament (Jer. 31:15).

An angel (or energy being) appeared to Jesus's earthly father, Joseph, and warned him to flee to Egypt. King Herod wanted Jesus dead because the prophecies described Jesus as the king of the Jews who was coming to rule. Herod was fearful for his kingship.

Joseph and his family stayed in Egypt till the king's death and then returned to their homeland.

As a grown man, Jesus came to John the Baptist (as was also prophesied in the Old Testament in Isaiah 40:3) in the wilderness. John was actually Jesus's cousin. Matthew 3:13 says, "Then Jesus came to Jordan unto John to be baptized by him." This happened in AD 27.

> And Jesus, when he was baptized, when out of the water, the heavens were opened, and he saw the Spirit of God descending like a dove, and lighting upon him, and a voice coming from heaven, saying, This is my beloved son in whom I am well pleased. (Luke 3:22; Mark 1;10; Matt. 3:16)

The next mention of one of these vehicles is five years later. Matthew 17 says,

> And after six days Jesus took Peter, James and John his brother, and brought them up into a high mountain, and Jesus was transfigured before them, and his face did shine [similar to when Moses returned from being in the cloud of the Lord for forty days on Mount Sinai 1,400 years previously] as the sun, and his raiment was white as the light, and behold, there appeared unto them Moses and Elijah talking with Jesus [Moses and Elijah had died 1,400 and 900 years previously] like old friends about Jesus's approaching death in Jerusalem. Then Peter said to Jesus, "Lord, it is good for us to be here, if you will, let us make three tabernacles, one for you, one for Moses and one for Elijah."

While he spoke, a bright cloud overshadowed them, and a voice came out of the cloud [similar to the events of Moses's time when God spoke to the ancient Israelites from out of the cloud], which said, "This is my beloved son, in whom I am well pleased, hear him."
And when the disciples heard it, they fell on their faces, and were afraid. Jesus came and touched them and said, "Arise, and don't be afraid." When they looked they saw no man but Jesus.
Moses and Elijah went with the cloud (energy vehicle).

The next mention of these clouds is in Matthew 24:27–30 around AD 33. This event is called the Olivet Discourse.

Jesus was on the Mount of Olives near Jerusalem, talking to his disciples about his return at the end of the age and the world situation at the time of the end of man's rule.

Immediately after the tribulation of those days shall the sun be darkened and the moon shall not give its light, and the stars shall fall from heaven [meteorites], and the power of the heavens shall be shaken.
And then shall appear the sign of the son of man [Jesus Christ] in heaven, and then shall all the tribes of the earth mourn, and they shall see the son of man coming in the clouds of heaven [the same way he left the earth] with power and great glory. (Matt. 24:30)

These clouds represent great power, much, much more than anything we have on earth. The misguided armies of the earth will attack the returning Jesus.

And he [Jesus] will send his angels [energy beings] with the sound of a trumpet, and they will gather together his elect [human beings chosen from throughout the ages, such as the disciples, who will number 144,002] from the four winds, from one end of heaven to the other. (Matt. 24:31)

A similar account is in Paul's letter to the church in Thessalonica (a Greek city) decades later, in AD 54, twenty years after Jesus's death and resurrection (1Thess. 4:14–18).

But I would not have you ignorant, brethren, concerning them which are asleep [dead] that you sorrow not, the same way others do who have no hope [atheists]. (1Thess. 4:13)

For if we believe that Jesus died and rose again, even so, then those also who sleep in Jesus [men and women who died chosen by Jesus] will God bring with him, for this we say unto you by the word of the Lord, that we who remain alive unto the coming of the Lord shall by no means precede those which are asleep.

For the Lord himself shall descend from heaven with a shout, with the voice of an archangel, and with the trump of God, and the dead chosen by Christ shall rise first.

Then we who are alive and remain shall be raised up together with them in the clouds [they shall be transported into these energy vehicles, which already contain the angels and the resurrected 144,002 elect who were chosen by Jesus Christ], to meet the Lord in the air [sky], and so shall we be always with the Lord.

Living and dead people from all over the world, from many different time periods, being transformed into spirit (energy beings or immortals) and being transported up into these energy vehicles, where Jesus and his angels (or energy beings) are already preparing to take over governing the planet, just before the governments of the world destroy it.

Jesus left this earth after his death and resurrection in one of these energy vehicles and is returning with many of these clouds according to these ancient writers.

CHAPTER 16

BOOK OF MATTHEW

Matthew 2:1–10 says, "Now when Jesus was born in Bethlehem, in King Herod's day, wise men from the east came to Jerusalem asking, 'Where is he that is born king of the Jews? For we have seen his star in the east and have come to worship him.'" King Herod was troubled upon hearing this (he feared for his kingship since he wasn't a Jew), and he asked the Jewish priests where Christ would be born. They replied he would be born in Bethlehem because it was written in the books of the prophets. Then Herod called the wise men and asked them when the star appeared, and he sent the wise men to Bethlehem to find the child for him, telling them he also wanted to worship the child. But he was planning to murder the child, thinking he was a danger to his rule.

The wise men left King Herod, and the star appeared. They followed it to Bethlehem, and it stopped above where the child was. Obviously, this was not a star like our sun. Many people mistakenly look for an actual star that might have glowed in Jesus's time. Similarly, Moses and the Israelites fourteen hundred years previously had followed a cloud by day and a fire by night. (The energy vehicle had been closer to the ground.)

The wise men rejoiced with "exceeding great joy" (Matt. 2:10–12). They went in to see the child and present gifts to the family, and then they left and returned to their homeland in the east without telling King Herod where the child was.

King Herod found out and responded by slaughtering the children under the age of two in the area, an event that was also prophesied in the Old Testament, in Jeremiah 31:15. An angel (or energy being) appeared to Jesus's earthly father, Joseph, and warned him to flee to Egypt. King Herod wanted Jesus dead because the prophecies described Jesus as the king of the Jews who was coming to rule. Herod was fearful for his kingship.

Joseph and his family stayed in Egypt until the king's death, and then they returned to his homeland. As a grown man, Jesus came to John the Baptist (as also prophesied in the Old Testament) in the wilderness (John was actually Jesus's cousin); see Matthew 3:13. Then Jesus came to Jordan to be baptized by John in AD 27. And when Jesus was baptized, the heavens were opened, and he saw the spirit of God descending like a dove. Lighting upon him, and he heard a voice coming from heaven, saying, "This is my beloved son, in whom I am well pleased."

The next mention of one of these "vehicles" is five years later, in 32 AD, as told in Matthew 17:

And after six days Jesus took Peter, James and John his brother, and brought them up into a high Mountain, and Jesus was transfigured before them, and his face did shine [similar to when Moses returned from being in the cloud of the Lord for forty days on Mount Sinai, fourteen hundred years previously] as the sun, and his raiment was white as the light, and behold, there appeared unto them Moses and Elijah talking with Jesus [Moses and Elijah died fourteen hundred and nine hundred years previously] like old friends about Jesus approaching death in Jerusalem. Then

Peter said to Jesus, "Lord, it is good for us to be here, if you will, let us make three tabernacles [tents], one for you, one for Moses and one for Elijah." While he spoke, a bright cloud [energy vehicle] overshadowed them, and a voice came out of the cloud [similar to the events of Moses time when God spoke to the Ancient Israelites from out of the cloud], which said, "This is my beloved son, in whom I am well pleased, hear [listen to] him." And when the disciples heard it, they fell on their faces, and were afraid [understandably so]. "Jesus came and touched them and said, Arise, and don't be afraid. When they looked they saw no man but Jesus." Moses and Elijah having gone with the cloud [energy vehicle].

The next mention is in Matthew 24, of the Olivet Discourse in 33 AD. Jesus is upon the Mount of Olives near Jerusalem, talking to his disciples about his return at the end of the age and the world situation at that time.

Immediately after the tribulation of those days shall the sun be darkened and the moon shall not give its light, and the stars shall fall from heaven [meteorites], and the power of the heavens shall be shaken. And then shall appear the sign of the son of man [Jesus Christ] in heaven, and then shall all the tribes of the earth mourn, and they shall see the son of man [Jesus Christ] coming in the clouds of heaven [the same way he left the earth] with power and great glory.

These clouds represent great power, much, much more than anything we have on earth. The misguided armies of the earth will attack the returning Jesus. And he (Jesus) will send his angels (energy beings) with the sound of a trumpet, and they will gather together his elect (those human beings chosen from throughout the ages such as the disciples, numbering 144,002) from the four winds, from one end of heaven to the other.

This was reinforced in Paul's letter to the church in Thessalonica (a Greek city) decades later, in AD 54, twenty years after Jesus death and resurrection chapter. See 1 Thessalonians 4:13–16:

> But I would not have you ignorant, brethren, concerning them which are asleep [dead] that you sorrow not, the same way others do who have no hope [atheists]. For if we believe that Jesus died and rose again, even so, then those also who sleep in Jesus [chosen by Jesus who died] will God bring with him, for this we say unto you by the word of the Lord, that we who remain alive unto the coming of the Lord shall by no means precede those which are asleep [dead]. For the Lord himself shall descend from heaven with a shout, with the voice of an Archangel, and with the trump of God, and the dead chosen by Christ shall rise first. Then we who are alive and remain shall be raised up together with them in the clouds [they shall be transported into these energy vehicles that already contain the angels and the resurrected elect chosen by Jesus Christ—144,002 individuals], to meet the Lord in the air [sky], and so shall we always be with the Lord.

Living and dead people from all over the world, from many different time periods, are being transformed into "spirit" (energy beings, immortals) and transported up into these energy vehicles clouds, where Jesus and his angels (energy beings) already are in preparation to take over governing the planet, just before the governments of the world destroy it. Jesus left this earth after his death and resurrection in one of these energy vehicles, and he is returning with many of them, according to these ancient writers.

Matthew 28 describes how Jesus Christ has been crucified and Mary Magdalene goes to his tomb near dawn: "And behold," there was a great earthquake, for an angel of the Lord descended from heaven, almost certainly in one of these clouds, and came and rolled back the stone from the door of the tomb and sat on it. His appearance was like "lightning" (energy) and his clothing white as snow. And the angel (energy being) tells the obviously terrified Mary to fear not, for Jesus, who was crucified, has risen from the dead.

Jesus then appears to his disciples and many others over a period of forty days and commands his disciples to be witnesses about his ministry and resurrection, first in Jerusalem, Judea, and Samaria and then to all the world.

And when he had spoken these things, while they looked, he was raised up into the sky and a cloud [energy vehicle] received him out of their sight. And while they looked up into the sky as Jesus went into the cloud [energy vehicle], behold: two men [energy beings] stood by them in white clothing, who said, "Men of Galilee, why do you stand looking up into the sky? This same Jesus, who is taken up from you into heaven [in the cloud-energy vehicle], shall come back in the same way as you saw him go into heaven. (Acts 1)

The Bible tells the story of an immortal being who is artificially inseminated into a female human being, Mary, wife of Joseph, and lives out a human existence since birth, experiencing all that human beings experience, including extreme pain at his scourging and crucifixion and human death, before being resurrected back into immortality. Quite a story—the most amazing story ever told, inadvertently confirmed by the relationship of these clouds of the Lord throughout humanity's history.

Many atheists throughout history and even today scoff at the suggestion of Mary giving birth as a virgin. With our current technology, it's not a big deal, for example through IVF. So why would it be unreasonable to believe this happened in Jesus's time, with the technology these beings obviously have? If they can visit earth from somewhere else in the universe, it would be a simple matter for them.

Clouds visiting Moses, clouds visiting Jesus, clouds taking the resurrected Jesus from the earth to the ruler of the universe (God)...clouds coming back to earth with Jesus and the angels to rule the earth and save humanity from itself. Clouds, clouds, clouds! Were these ancient people *obsessed* with clouds? Did they have the intelligence and will to deceive future generations by lying about these clouds? Or have they just reported what they saw, what they heard, and what they were told by Jesus and these energy beings?

Throughout all the religious confusion, with thousands of differing doctrines from thousands of differing churches and religions, the clouds of the Lord reveal something *extraordinary.*

You can be an intelligent, educated person and believe that we are not alone on this planet. I believe there is a president of the United States of America because I have much tangible evidence of him, even though I have never seen him personally. I also believe in these energy beings for many of the same reasons—there is evidence of their existence and their vehicles and other knowledge that is contained in the Bible and other independent sources.

CHAPTER 17

BOOK OF MARK

M ark's account of Jesus Christ meeting John the Baptist, who was Jesus's cousin, born to Elizabeth (Jesus's aunt) in her old age.

And it came to pass, in those days, that Jesus came from Nazareth, in Galilee, and was baptized by John in Jordan. And after coming up out of the water, he saw the heavens opened and the spirit like a dove descending on him. And there came a voice from heaven (the sky), saying, "You are my beloved son, in whom I am well pleased." This is a similar description to the cloud. The sky opening suggests an entry from another dimension, possibly something similar to a wormhole.

This event happened around AD 27, at the beginning of Jesus Christ's ministry and the end of John the Baptist's.

Mark's account of the Transfiguration of Jesus Christ is in chapter 9:2–8, near the end of Christ's ministry, around AD 32.

And after six days, Jesus took with him Peter, James, and John and led them up into a high mountain apart by themselves.

And he was transfigured before them, and his raiment became shining, exceeding white as snow, so as no fuller on earth can whiten them, and there appeared unto them Elijah and Moses and they were talking with Jesus, and Peter answered and said to Jesus, "It is good for us to be here, let us make three tabernacles (tents), one for you, one for Moses and one for Elijah," for he did not know what to say for they were very afraid.

And there was a cloud that overshadowed them, and a voice came out of the cloud saying, "This is my beloved son, hear him."

Once again, the voice came from the cloud. Have you ever heard before that a voice came from a cloud? The significance of this cloud has been missed by the world, for it is not a rain cloud but an energy vehicle, which is far, far superior to our helicopters, planes, spaceships, or anything else on earth.

"And suddenly when they looked around they saw no man except Jesus" (Mark 9:8). The cloud left with Moses and Elijah. Similar descriptions are in Matthew 17 and Luke 9, but they aren't exactly the same, showing no collusion.

Mark's account of the Olivet Discourse on the Mount of Olives outside Jerusalem, in AD 33.

Jesus Christ told his disciples about conditions in the world prior to his second coming: "And then shall they see the son of man coming in the clouds of heaven with great power and glory. And then shall he send his angels, and he shall gather together his elect [those chosen by Jesus to rule the planet under him who have been selected throughout the ages] from the four winds, from the uttermost parts of the earth to the uttermost parts of heaven" (Mark 13:26–27).

People being gathered by these energy beings on Jesus Christ's behalf from all over the earth.

Other parts of the Bible reveal that even those who have been long dead are being chosen, resurrected, and beamed up or raised up into these clouds, and they are being transformed into immortals, the same as the angels, who don't need to breathe or eat and are impervious to heat. Can this be accurate and true?

Let's look at Mark's account of Jesus Christ's arrest just before his crucifixion, later in AD 33.

Jesus appeared before the Jewish high priest and the chief priests (after Judas's betrayal for thirty pieces of silver [Mark 14:10]). The high priest asked Jesus Christ, "Are you the Christ [the messiah] the son of the blessed?"

And Jesus replied, "I am, and you shall see the son of man sitting on the right hand of power and coming in the clouds of heaven."

Upon hearing this, the high priest demanded Jesus's execution and sent him to Pontius Pilate (the Roman governor) because the execution had to be approved by the ruling Roman authorities.

Jesus talked about his future return in the clouds of heaven while he was on trial for his life.

Jesus talked about coming with power in the clouds just before his crucifixion.

These clouds represent much power, as described in the Psalms: "God's strength is in his clouds (Psalm 68:34).

The clouds that the ancient Israelites witnessed in the days of Moses, Solomon, Elijah, and others have had a profound effect on all their witnesses.

A proper understanding of these clouds, called clouds of heaven, clouds of the Lord, chariots of fire, lights from heaven, and so on, helps to make these ancient writings easier to understand and allows the reader to see that Bible passages are not fables. The apostle Peter said in AD 66, "We have not followed cunningly devised fables" (2 Pet. 1:16). This was thirty years after Christ's death and resurrection.

In other words, he says this is all real—the Bible's stories are not a fairy tale.

By studying the interactions of these clouds, it becomes easy to realize that these ancient writers have inadvertently revealed humanity's involvement with superior beings and far superior technology.

What these beings (energy beings) have told these ancient writers is even more astounding, combined with what the being referred to as Jesus Christ is reported to have said in the scriptures. The immortal (Jesus) who lived with us as a mortal two thousand years ago. The real story written in these scriptures is quite different from the general stories that are normally preached in churches (which do sound like fables).

Have you ever heard that Jesus Christ is returning to earth in an energy vehicle (cloud of the Lord)? So obvious once you know how to analyze the evidence properly. There is no need to rely on university professors, who themselves have been indoctrinated into a false belief system of what the Bible means and says.

The self-declared wise people who have stated the Bible is a collection of fables written by primitive, superstitious men have revealed themselves to be quite foolish, as these scriptures say, "The fool says in his heart there is no God" and " by declaring themselves wise they have become fools" (Psalm 14:1).

Anyone can make a mistake, but it takes a mature person to admit it.

Just like Albert Einstein, who is considered to be one of the most intelligent people to have ever lived. When he saw evidence that the universe had a beginning—just as the "primitive" writers of the Bible stated in Genesis 1:1 ("In the beginning, God created the heavens [universe] and the earth")—he admitted his blunder, which he referred to as the biggest blunder of his career, his cosmological constant.

Don't make the same blunder. Einstein had the information that the universe had a beginning previously, but because the intelligent elite of the world said the universe was always there, he didn't believe the evidence till he found it to be irrefutable.

One of the last statements recorded from Jesus Christ was that his gospel must be preached worldwide in all nations, and then the end of this age would come, and the age of Jesus Christ's return and rule of the earth with his chosen ones would begin (Matt. 24:31).

Preaching to the entire world is now coming to completion with the Internet and satellite TV.

By this fact and other related prophecies, we know there is not a lot of time left, but all of the biblical prophecies about this matter have to be fulfilled. Some are in their final stages, and some still need to occur.

World War III, without divine interference, would result in the deaths of all human beings.

Looking at the progression of death and destruction from World War I to World War II, it is very obvious that the level of death and destruction caused by World War III would be absolutely devastating on a horrific scale.

The amount of money being spent worldwide on developing peace as opposed to the amount of money being spent on war capabilities is extremely favorable to war winning out. Only a small percentage is being spent on peace.

The name of the United Nations would be more accurate if it were the Ununited Nations.

The United Nations is made up of most of the nations on the earth, including the most powerful—the United States, Russia, China, Britain, and France. The United Nations hasn't even been able to stop wars and mass killings in some of the weakest nations on this planet, such as Rwanda, Congo, and many others.

Because all that the Bible records happening in the past and present has occurred or is occurring, we can be confident that future events recorded in the scriptures will also occur.

CHAPTER 18

THE GOSPEL OF LUKE

There was in the days of Herod, the king of Judea, a certain priest named Zacharias and his wife Elizabeth, and they had no children because Elizabeth was barren, and they were both stricken with age.

And it came to pass when Zacharias was performing his priestly duty in the temple, there appeared to him an Angel of the Lord standing on the right side of the altar.

And when Zacharias saw him he was terrified, but the Angel said to him, "Fear not, Zacharias, your prayers have been heard, and your wife Elizabeth shall bear a son, and you shall call him John. (Luke 1:5)

This baby was John the Baptist. Zacharias told the angel that he and his wife were way too old to bear a child, and the angel (energy being) said he was Gabriel, who stands before God (Luke 1:19).

Six months later, the being Gabriel went to a virgin named Mary, who was living in the town of Nazareth, and said, "Fear not, you will have a child and name him Jesus, and he shall be great and come to rule forever." Mary said to Gabriel, "How can this be when I have not known a man [had sex]?" (Luke 1:34).

Gabriel told her that God would artificially inseminate her (for want of a better term) with the Holy Spirit, that her elderly cousin Elizabeth was already six months pregnant in spite of her old age, and that nothing was impossible with God (Luke 1:36).

There is no mention of the location of the cloud Gabriel came in this chapter, but Luke 2:8 mentions the glory of the Lord appearing to shepherds: "And there was in the same country, shepherds abiding in the fields, keeping watch over their flock by night, and lo, the angel of the Lord came upon them, and the glory of the Lord shone round about them, and they were very afraid." The glory shining around the shepherds is a similar description to the cloud of the Lord.

And the angel said to the shepherds, "Fear not" (Luke 2:11), and told them the Savior had been born in the city of David (Bethlehem).

The shepherds went to Bethlehem and found Mary, Joseph, and the baby lying in a manger.

And the shepherds told everyone what the angel said, and Mary called the baby Jesus as Gabriel told them to before the child was conceived.

Elizabeth, who was an old woman, and Mary, who was a virgin, conceived and delivered with the technology Gabriel provided two thousand years ago. We have only had that technology for a few decades, yet these ancient people reported it two thousand years ago.

The technology came from these angels, who came to earth in these clouds, and yet some supposedly wise people state the Bible and science don't mix. The Bible, even though it's not a science textbook, is full of sound scientific principles.

The story of Adam and Eve—read it yourself in Genesis. I'll give you a scientific translation in modern terms.

Genesis 2:21 says that God anaesthetized Adam, performed an operation on him, took out one of his ribs, and closed up the flesh again, and God used the rib to clone a woman. And Adam called her Eve.

That is what that passage is essentially saying. Nearly six thousand years later, we are beginning to clone ourselves. The Bible is full of scientific principles, when correctly understood. You don't need an Oxford degree to see this.

The reason for the scientific principles in the Bible is that these angels (or energy beings) have a deep understanding of science.

The sanitation and isolation guidelines in the book of Leviticus have long been considered sound scientific principles that were well advanced for their time.

Some of these sanitary principles have only been included in our western society in the last 150 years, but the ancients were told about them in the time of Moses, 3,500 years ago.

The practice of these laws has saved millions of people and could have saved many millions more.

The next mention of Jesus Christ is when Jesus is about thirty years old. Luke 3:1 says,

Now in the fifteenth year of Tiberius Caesar, Pontius Pilate being governor of Judea, and Herod being Tetrarch of Iturea, John the Baptist is preaching in the wilderness about the coming kingdom of God.

Now when all the people were baptized, it came to pass that Jesus, also being baptized and praying, the heavens were opened, and the holy ghost descended in bodily shape like a dove upon him, and a voice came from heaven, which said, "Thou art my beloved son, in whom I am well pleased."

Luke 3 is similar to but not exactly the same as Matthew's and Mark's accounts, showing no collusion to deceive people.

CHAPTER 19
ACTS OF THE APOSTLES

After Jesus Christ was crucified and resurrected from the dead, he appeared, walked, talked, and ate with his disciples for forty days (Acts 1:3).

At the end of the forty days, Acts 1:8 says,

> But you [the apostles] shall receive power, after the Holy Ghost is come upon you.
> You shall be witnesses about me in Jerusalem, in Judea and Samaria and to the uttermost parts of the earth.
> And when he had spoken these things, while they looked, he was taken up into the sky, and a cloud received him out of their sight.

These are the same clouds that visited Moses and Elijah fifteen hundred and one thousand years previously, that Moses and Elijah came in to visit Jesus not long before his crucifixion, and that the Israelites followed in the wilderness and under which they passed through the sea; they're the same clouds in which God visited the finished tabernacle in the desert with Moses, the same clouds that visited the finished temple of Solomon, that

Jesus said he would return to earth to govern the earth with power and glory, and the same clouds mentioned in the book of Psalms: "God's strength is in his clouds, who makes these clouds his chariots."

These clouds are not rain clouds; they are energy vehicles that the immortal energy beings make their chariots.

The ancient writers used these terms to describe what they witnessed, and the angels also used these terms so these primitive people could understand the Angels.

These clouds are vehicles used by these beings, whom the ancient writers refer to as God and angels.

The next chapters refer to Jesus Christ's return to earth.

Acts 1:10 says, "And while they looked steadfastly toward heaven as he went up into the sky, behold, two men stood by them in white apparel [angels], who said, 'You men of Galilee, why stand you gazing up into heaven, this same Jesus, who is taken up from you into heaven, shall come back the same way you saw him go into heaven.'"

Jesus left the earth after his resurrection in a cloud, coming back to the earth in a cloud.

This being we refer to as Jesus Christ told his disciples to witness his resurrection to the whole world, which is precisely what has happened; the rest is history. In spite of all the confusion in the many diverse churches, all Christians believe in Christ's resurrection—Catholics, Protestants, Orthodox, and so on.

Since we do not have the ability today to resurrect those who are truly dead, the technology that brought Jesus Christ back to life after he was dead for three days two thousand years ago came from an otherworldly source, which the ancient writers inadvertently revealed as coming from the angels who came to Jesus Christ's tomb in a cloud.

It is obvious that something spectacular happened two thousand years ago in Jerusalem that has affected the whole world.

It's also obvious that something spectacular happened thirty-five hundred years ago in the Middle East in Moses's time, which still has a profound effect upon the Jews and Muslims and Christians of the world.

Today, thousands of years later, with the help of scientific reasoning and by applying unbiased logic, we can determine what happened much more clearly than those who were alive during the Dark and Middle Ages, and we don't have to rely on the educated elite. We can investigate for ourselves. The educated elite of the Middle Ages hid the knowledge in the Bible by keeping it in the language of the elite—Latin. Translating the Bible into another language, or even possessing a Bible that had been translated (or any piece of scripture not written in Latin), would likely have resulted in horrific torture and being burnt at the stake (read the story of Jan Hus burnt alive) (Wikipedia: http://en.wikipedia.org/wiki/Jan_Hus).

Many of the educated elite of today are also misleading the masses, ridiculing the Bible, God, and anyone who does not hold on to their unrealistic views.

Many people died horrible deaths to allow everyone access to this book, the Bible. So why not see whether what they died for has something to offer you (besides a horrible death at the stake).

CHAPTER 20

THE CONVERSION OF
SAUL (OR PAUL)

In Acts 9:1, Paul talks about beating and slaughtering the disciples of Jesus after his crucifixion. He went to the Jewish high priest and asked him for letters to take to synagogues in Damascus (Syria) to get help arresting the followers of Jesus and bringing them to Jerusalem for judgment. He was a fanatical Jew, willing to even kill for his religious beliefs.

As he journeyed, he came near Damascus, and suddenly there shone round about him a light from heaven, and he panicked, and he heard a voice say to him, "Saul, Saul, why do you persecute me?"

And Saul said, "Who are you, Lord?"

"I am Jesus," replied the voice.

The rest is history. This Jewish fanatic became one of the staunchest Christians of all time.

A light from heaven, a cloud of the Lord, the chariots of God, or my personal term—*energy vehicle*—I believe none of these descriptions are satisfactorily accurate.

Nearly thirty years after his conversion, Paul recounted the events that changed him from a Christian-persecuting fanatic to a staunch supporter of Jesus Christ, after being arrested and brought to account before the king, Agrippa, and the Roman governor.

Acts 26:13 says, "At midday, O King, I saw in the way a light from heaven, above the brightness of the sun shining round about us."

And then Paul recounts Jesus Christ talking to him.

1 Corinthians 10:1–2 says, "Moreover, brethren, I don't want you to be ignorant of the fact that all our fathers were under the cloud [energy vehicle], and they all passed through the divided sea on dry land, with the waters standing up on their left and right sides [a force field from the cloud that held the waters back for the Israelites to cross]. And they were all baptized with Moses in the cloud and in the sea." The Egyptians drowned behind them in the collapsing waters as the force field disappeared.

Paul inadvertently revealed the cloud parting the sea (this is not mentioned in the Old Testament), with Moses and the Israelites crossing through the sea under the cloud. The cloud, which is not mentioned in this particular act in the Old Testament, makes the Old Testament account more understandable. The energy vehicle parted the sea and used a force field to hold back the water for the Israelites to cross underneath it.

Paul's letter to the church in Thessalonica says,

> But I don't want you to be ignorant, brethren, concerning them which are asleep [dead], that you have hope, for if we believe that Jesus died and rose again, then those who sleep in Jesus, God will bring with him.
>
> For the Lord himself shall descend from heaven with a shout, and the dead in Christ [the elect or chosen ones] shall rise first.
>
> Then we which are alive at that time shall be raised up to-gether with those already in the clouds and we shall stay with the Lord. (1 Thess. 4:13–17)

When Jesus Christ was alive, he said he would return in these clouds of heaven with power and glory (1 Thess. 4:17).

When Jesus ascended to heaven, he went into one of these clouds (Acts 1:9).

While the apostles watched Jesus go up into the sky into the cloud, two angels told them he would come back the same way (in a cloud) (Acts 1;:10–11).

Living and dead people being raised up (or beamed up) into these clouds of heaven where the returning Jesus Christ and his angels are.

CHAPTER 21

BOOK OF REVELATION

The book of Revelation—the last book of the Bible—was written by John, Jesus Christ's last living apostle, around AD 96. John was imprisoned on the Isle of Patmos by the Roman authorities for his preaching.

Revelation begins with the revelation of the resurrected Jesus Christ, which God gave to him to show his servants things that must happen, and he sent it to his disciple John.

John sent the revelations to the seven churches in Asia.

From Jesus Christ, who is the first to be raised from the dead, who is immortal, who is to return to earth (Rev. 1:5):

Behold he comes with clouds and everyone shall see him.

John was commanded to write down the things he had seen (the past), the things which are (the present), and the things to come (the future).

John went on to write about a future period in time, which sounds much like today, with unusual seismic activity, weather conditions, and wars. This time period will culminate in one-third of the earth's population being destroyed.

God says to the sixth angel, "Loose the four angels which are bound in the Euphrates [the main river in Iraq]" (Rev. 9:14). And goes on to describe massive armies involved in warfare destroying the third part of humanity (Rev. 9:14–15).

The Iraq War has set off events that have made the world a much more volatile place, increasing Islamic extremism and anti-West attitudes across the globe.

The next chapter, Revelation 10:1, says, "And I saw another mighty angel come down from heaven, clothed with a cloud, and a rainbow was upon his head, and his face was as it were the sun, and his feet as pillars of fire." This is a description of an energy being and a description of future events that John saw in a vision, which was apparently beamed into his eyes or mind, like a movie.

Human vision technology is only in its infancy today.

Then in Revelation 11:4 John hears, "And I will give power to my two witnesses [of God and Jesus Christ], and they shall prophesy one thousand, two hundred and sixty days."

They (the two witnesses) shall then be killed in Jerusalem at the end of this period (Rev. 11:7–8), and their dead bodies will lie in the street for three and a half days; after this time, the two witnesses will be resurrected, and a voice from heaven will say to them to come up, and they will ascend up to heaven into a cloud (Rev. 11:12). This happens when Jesus Christ returns to the earth with his angels in the clouds of heaven, and the elect (the chosen ones of Jesus Christ) will also be brought into the returning clouds. This is similar to an account in Paul's letter to the Thessalonians about Christ's return.

Then we who are alive and remain shall be brought up (beamed up) to those who are already in the cloud (the resurrected dead, Jesus Christ, and his angels) in the sky (1 Thess. 4:17).

The ancient writers inadvertently revealed interactions with beings who have fantastic technology and who claim they can resurrect the dead, even if their bodies have decomposed completely, and make them immortal with new bodies that time and the elements have no effect on.

I would imagine if you have read this book (clouds of the Lord) and studied and checked to see whether it is true, you would make the logical assumption that humanity has had interactions with beings of much higher intelligence than ours.

So who are they? Are they aliens from another planet or humans from the future?

CHAPTER 22
WHO DO THEY SAY THEY ARE?

The Gospel (good news) according to John says, "In the beginning was the Word and the Word was with God. All things were made by him" (John 1:1–2). *The Word* is a title for Jesus Christ, and the statement that he made all things says Jesus was involved in creating the universe.

Genesis 1:1 says, "In the beginning God created the heavens and the earth...The sixth day, God said, 'Let us make man in our own image, and let him rule over the whole earth.'"

Genesis 2:7 says, "And the Lord God formed a man out of the dust of the earth [most likely genetic material, such as bone, to make our current species] and breathed into him the breath of life." Then God placed the man in a garden called Eden, in modern-day Iraq. As our creators, God and Jesus Christ refer to themselves as our father and his son, our older and much-wiser brother. They offer humans the chance to join them as immortals, if we will accept them as such and follow their guidance. That's the primary message in the Gospel (good news). We have the offer of immortality from these beings. As I said in the beginning of *Clouds of the Lord* in the "Old Testament" section.

The clouds of the Lord is only one area of the consistency and accuracy of the Bible; many so-called Bible scholars and preachers have little understanding of the Bible. You can check all the information written here in clouds of the Lord and see whether it is correct. Do not blindly believe the supposed experts. The Bible itself warns against these so-called wise men and describes them as fools (Rom. 1:21–22).

Another statement in the Bible says, "I am God and there is none like me, declaring the end from the beginning, and from ancient times things not yet done" (Isa. 46:9–10). The Bible that is in existence today is no amazing coincidence; it was declared from ancient times to reach us today, to give us guidance and hope.

The Bible is full of statements that are similar to Isaiah 46:9, intended for the scoffers, particularly the ones who write these misleading books that state that the Bible is a collection of fables by primitive humans and that anyone who believes it is backward. This verse in particular says, "The fool says in his heart 'there is no God,' and by professing themselves to be wise [by writing these misleading books] they have become fools" (Rom. 1:22).

I'm not saying this; God did, thousands of years ago. You can believe this book or you can believe the writers of these misleading books (which ridicule the Bible). They are the primitive humans writing fables, not the Bible writers.

My advice is to make up your own mind. These misleading books (which ridicule the Bible) actually help to confirm the authenticity of the Bible, which says, "In the last days, scoffers will come, saying, 'Where is he [Jesus Christ]?'" Things (life) go on as they always have (2 Pet. 3:3–4).

So if there were no scoffers, then the verse about scoffers would not be accurate.

These misleading writers inadvertently help to authenticate the Bible. It can be quite hard to believe the Bible without the correct information and the part about the clouds of the Lord, but a thorough investigation reveals time and again the same answer: interaction with supernatural (or superintelligent) beings who ultimately want us to join them as immortals. Perhaps the Bible really is correct, and if it is, it is certainly worth investigating personally. Your choice: investigate, yourself. You do not need to have Harvard or Oxford degrees to study the Bible.

When I was at school in the 1960s and 1970s, I was told that the universe is endless and has always existed. Albert Einstein (one of the greatest physicists of all time) believed this to be so in spite of his calculations and genius. When he found out the universe had a beginning and was not static, he called his mistake (cosmological constant) the biggest blunder of his career.

We now know the universe had a beginning about fourteen billion years ago (the Big Bang) and that everything is travelling through the universe at enormous speed; the earth is travelling through space around the sun at sixty-seven thousand miles per hour.

Imagine a balloon being continually inflated to enormous size and that everything in the universe is contained within this balloon.

Genesis 1:1 says, "In the beginning God created the heavens [universe] and the earth."

The Bible stated thousands of years ago that the universe had a beginning, whereas the intellectual elite of the nineteenth and early twentieth centuries said the universe had no beginning, that it had always been there. Even Albert Einstein fell for this deception, calling it the biggest blunder of his career.

What's at the central point where the universe started? Revelation 20:11 says, "And I saw a great white throne, and him that sat on it, from whom the earth and the heavens fled away."

The earth and the universe are moving quickly away from God, which is to be expected because the creator of the universe, whose throne seems to be at the center of the entire universe, created the universe from there fourteen billion years ago.

There is enormous evidence of design throughout the earth and the entire universe; understanding the role of the clouds of the Lord will help you understand some of the genius of the designers of the earth.

These beings reveal to us that all creation is our ultimate inheritance for all eternity (Matt. 25:34).

We will not be allowed to conquer the universe till we conquer our defects of character.

CHAPTER 23

WHAT IS GOD'S ULTIMATE PLAN?

U ltimately the Bible states that God is not content with the way things are on the earth and has set a plan in motion for God himself to come here and live among us, his children. The first time Jesus Christ officially came to earth two thousand years ago was to announce the coming kingdom of God and to set in motion the recruitment of 144,002 humans from throughout history to help Jesus Christ rule at his second coming (which will occur just in the nick of time before humanity destroys itself).

This period will last for one thousand years (Rev. 20:1–15), and humanity will be refined to be suitable for immortality. In other words, humans will have the choice to join the kingdom as sons and daughters of the creator. Once the incorrigibly wicked choose euthanasia over change, there will be no more evil, and God will live and rule among us, opening up the universe for us to sub-due and be caretakers of (God wants us to be good caretakers of the earth first). Everyone who ever lived will have that choice. The Bible talks about a second resurrection after the one thousand years of Christ's rule; God states he doesn't want to lose anyone and implores humans to accept his offer of eternal life and love (1 John 2:25).

The concept in the Bible that the good go to heaven and the bad go to hell is misguided and misleading. The Bible does not state this at all; this is a doctrine of man. God is coming to the earth one thousand years after Christ begins his direct rule from Jerusalem—the future capital of the world and eventually the capital of the entire galaxy and then the universe.

CHAPTER 24

EVENTS OF THE LAST GENERATION

- Atomic bomb, 1945: their flesh being consumed while they were still standing, eyes and tongue drying up—heat blast from atomic bomb (Zech. 14:12).
- Establishment of Jewish state, 1948: becoming the center of world conflict.
- A single entity is going to control the world's finances (Rev. 13:17).
- Sputnik, 1957: worldwide communication to see the returning Christ (Rev. 1:7).
- Population explosion to support the 200-million-man armies: Revelation talks about this massive force crossing the Euphrates River to attack the armies already in the Middle East. At this point, Christ will return; the armies will attack Christ, believing him to be their enemy; the armies of the world will be destroyed; and this will usher in a one-thousand-year period of peace and growth. When these prophecies of a 200-million-man army was written, the estimated population of the entire world was about 150

million. How did John know that a population explosion
would come in the last days that could field such a huge
force east of the Euphrates River (east of Iraq) in countries
such as Iran (population 75 million), Pakistan (population
183 million), India (population 1.27 billion), and of course,
China (population 1.303 billion)? Only in this current generation is such a large force possible.

All this information Inadvertently reveals vehicles of extreme
levels of technology, which is to be expected of beings who
are able to visit the earth from anywhere else in this universe, owing to the extreme distances and hazards of such a journey from
outer space or from another dimension.

The Bible writers' descriptions of events past, present, and future fit into a pattern of logic that is well beyond the many writers
from many different ancient time periods to collude on and falsify.

So much so that any rational, logical, thinking person today with
any reasonable amount of intelligence would have to concede is based
on facts. In other words, if you are intelligent enough to read this
page and understand what is written on this page, you have enough
intelligence to understand the rest of this book. You don't have to be
a university professor at Oxford or Harvard. You only need to slightly
open your mind and to have a tiny amount of humility.

What is the purpose of these beings who visit our planet in
these clouds and chariots? According to these ancient writers (who
wrote the Bible), the answer will impact every human being who
has ever lived. Read on, and make up your own mind.

These clouds represent great power, much, much more than
anything we have on the earth. The misguided armies of the earth
will attack the returning Jesus.

And he [Jesus] will send his angels [energy beings] with the
sound of a trumpet, and they will gather together his elect

[human beings chosen from throughout the ages, such as Jesus's disciples, who will number 144,002] from the four winds, from one end of heaven to the other.

Reinforced in Paul's letter to the church in Thessalonica (a Greek city) decades later, in AD 54, twenty years after Jesus's death and resurrection (3:13):

But I would not have you ignorant, brethren, concerning them which are asleep [dead] that you sorrow not, the same way others do who have no hope [atheists].
For if we believe that Jesus died and rose again, even so, then those also who sleep in Jesus [chosen by Jesus who died] will God bring with him, for this we say unto you by the word of the Lord, that we who remain alive unto the coming of the Lord shall by no means precede those which are asleep.
"For the Lord himself shall descend from heaven with a shout, with the voice of an archangel, and with the trump of God, and the dead chosen by Christ shall rise first.
Then we who are alive and remain shall be raised up together with them in the clouds [they shall be transported into these energy vehicles, which already contain the angels and the resurrected 144,002 elect who were chosen by Jesus Christ], to meet the Lord in the air [sky], and so shall we be always with the Lord.

Living and dead people from all over the world, from many different time periods, being transformed into spirit (energy beings or immortals) and being transported up into these energy vehicles, where Jesus and his angels (or energy beings) are already preparing to take over governing the planet, just before the governments of the world destroy it.

Jesus left this earth after his death and resurrection in one of these energy vehicles and is returning with many of them, according to these ancient writers.

In Matthew 28, Jesus Christ has been crucified, and Mary Magdalene goes to his tomb near dawn. "And behold, there was a great earthquake, for an angel of the Lord descended from heaven [almost certainly in a cloud] and came and rolled back the stone from the door of the tomb and sat on it. His appearance was like lightning [energy] and his clothing white as snow" (Rev. 28:3). And the angel (energy being) tells the obviously terrified Mary not to fear Jesus, who was crucified and has risen from the dead. Jesus then appears to his disciples and many others over a period of forty days, and he commands his disciples to be witnesses about his ministry and resurrection, first in Jerusalem, Judea, and Samaria, and then to all the world.

> And when he had spoken these things, while they looked, he was raised up into the sky and a cloud (energy vehicle) received him out of their sight. And while they looked up into the sky as Jesus went into the cloud (energy vehicle), behold, two men (energy beings), stood by them in white clothing, who said, "Men of Galilee, why do you stand looking up into the sky? This same Jesus, who is taken up from you into heaven (in the cloud or energy vehicle) shall come back in the same way as you saw him go into heaven." (Acts 1:11)

An immortal being was artificially inseminated into Mary, a female human being, and lived out a human existence from birth, experiencing all that human beings experience, including extreme pain during his scourging and crucifixion, human death, and then resurrection into immortality. This is quite a story, the most amazing story ever told, and it's inadvertently confirmed by the relationship of these clouds of the Lord throughout humanity's history. Many atheists throughout history and even today scoff at the suggestion of Mary giving birth as a virgin; with our current IVF technology, it's not a big deal; so why would it be unreasonable to believe this happened in Jesus's time with the technology these beings obviously had? If they could visit the earth from somewhere else in the universe, it would be a simple matter for them.

Clouds visited Moses, Solomon, and Jesus, and clouds took the resurrected Jesus from the earth to the ruler of the universe (God). Clouds will come back to the earth with Jesus and the angels to rule the earth and save humanity from itself. Clouds, clouds, clouds—were these ancient people obsessed with clouds? Did they have the intelligence and will to deceive future generations by lying about these clouds? Or did they just report what they saw, what they heard, and what they were told by Jesus and these energy beings? Throughout all the religious confusion, with thousands of differing doctrines from thousands of differing churches and religions, the clouds of the Lord reveal something extraordinary. You can be an intelligent, educated person and believe in the fact we are not alone on this planet. I believe there is a president of the United States because I have much tangible evidence of his existence, even though I have never seen him personally. I also believe in these energy beings for many of the same reasons—the evidence of their existence is revealed here, and their vehicles and other knowledge contained in the Bible and other independent sources.

The reason for the scientific principles in the Bible is that these angels (or energy beings) have a deep understanding of science.

The sanitation and isolation guidelines in the book of Leviticus have long been considered sound scientific principles that were well advanced for their time.

Some of these have only been included in our western society in the past 150 years, but the ancients were told about them in the time of Moses, 3,500 years ago.

The practice of these laws has saved millions of people and could have saved many millions more.

The next mention of Jesus Christ is when Jesus is about thirty years old. Luke 3 says, Now in the fifteenth year of Tiberius Caesar, Pontius Pilate being governor of Judea, and Herod being Tetrarch of Iturea, John the Baptist is preaching in the wilderness about the coming kingdom of God.

Now when all the people were baptized, it came to pass that Jesus, also being baptized and praying, the heavens were opened, and the holy ghost descended in bodily shape like a dove upon him, and a voice came from heaven, which said, "Thou art my beloved son, in whom I am well pleased.

Luke 3 is similar to but not exactly the same as Matthew's and Mark's accounts, showing no collusion to deceive people.

Luke's account of the Transfiguration of Christ is found in 9:27: "But I tell you of a truth, there be some standing here which shall not taste of death till they see the kingdom of God." This occurs when the apostles see the resurrected Moses and Elijah and later the resurrection of Jesus himself and hear the very voice of God.

And it came to pass about eight days after Jesus had spoken of his execution and resurrection, he took Peter, John, and James and went up upon a mountain to pray. And as he prayed, the fashion of his countenance was altered, and his raiment was white and glistening. And behold, there talked with him two men, which were Moses and Elijah (both had died many centuries before and had interactions with clouds, whirlwinds, and chariots, also known as energy vehicles) who appeared in glory (as resurrected beings) and spoke of Jesus Christ's coming death, which he should accomplish in Jerusalem. But Peter and the others were heavy with sleep, and when they awoke, they saw his glory and the two men who stood with him. And it came to pass, as they departed from him, Peter said to Jesus, "Master, it is good for us to be here, let us make three tabernacles, one for you, one for Moses and one for Elijah, not knowing what to say." While he spoke, there came a cloud, which overshadowed them, and they were afraid when Jesus, Moses, and Elijah went into the cloud. And there came a voice out of the cloud, saying, "This is my beloved son, listen to him."

The same voice Moses had heard coming out of the cloud on Mount Sinai almost fifteen centuries earlier. And when the voice was past, they saw Jesus alone; God, Moses, and Elijah had gone with the cloud. As Jesus told his disciples, some of them—Peter, John, and James—saw the coming kingdom of God when they witnessed Moses and Elijah alive with the cloud and heard God's voice. The return of the Lord, Jesus Christ, in glory. Luke 21 says, "And there shall be signs in the sun, and in the moon, and in the stars, and upon the earth much trouble with the nations, with the sea and the oceans roaring. Men's hearts failing for fear [meaning very, very scary times] because of the terrible things which are happening on the earth. And then shall they see the son of man [Jesus Christ] coming in a cloud with great power and glory." The second coming of Jesus Christ in these clouds is reinforced in the book of Revelation, which was written about AD 96 by Jesus Christ's last living disciple, John, on the Roman penal isle of Patmos. "Behold he cometh with clouds and everyone shall see him, even those who pierced him." The Internet and satellite TV have now made it possible for the entire world to see the returning Christ in these clouds. One account of Jesus Christ returning to the earth in these clouds when he was alive on the earth in AD 33, and John wrote another account thirty-odd years later after Christ's resurrection, with the risen Christ revealing to John that he is coming back to the earth in these clouds. All with no sign of collusion or fabrication on the part of Luke or John. As hard as it can be to believe all this, it makes so much sense when put into its right context, as opposed to the fairy tales that abound with many religious denominations.

Acts 1:10 says, "And while they looked steadfastly toward heaven as he went up into the sky, behold, two men stood by them in white apparel [angels], who said, 'You men of Galilee, why stand you gazing up into heaven, this same Jesus, who is taken up from you into heaven, shall come back the same way you saw him go into heaven.'"

Left earth after his resurrection in a cloud, coming back to earth in a cloud.

This being we refer to as Jesus Christ told his disciples to witness his resurrection to the whole world, which is precisely what has happened; the rest is history. In spite of all the confusion in the many diverse churches, all Christians believe in Christ's resurrection—Catholics, Protestants, Orthodox, and so on.

Since we do not have the ability today to resurrect those who are truly dead, the technology that brought Jesus Christ back to life after he was dead for three days two thousand years ago came from an otherworldly source, which the ancient writers inadvertently revealed as coming from the angels who came to Jesus Christ's tomb in a cloud.

It is obvious that something spectacular happened two thousand years ago in Jerusalem that has affected the whole world.

It's also obvious that something spectacular happened thirty-five hundred years ago in the Middle East in Moses's time, which still has a profound effect upon the Jews and Muslims and Christians of the world.

Today, thousands of years later, with the help of scientific reasoning and by applying unbiased logic, we can determine what happened much more clearly than those who were alive during the Dark and Middle Ages, and we don't have to rely on the educated elite. We can investigate for ourselves. The educated elite of the Middle Ages hid the knowledge in the Bible by keeping it in the language of the elite—Latin. Translating the Bible into another language, or even possessing a Bible that had been translated (or any piece of scripture not written in Latin) would likely have resulted in horrific torture and being burnt at the stake (read the story of Jan Hus on *Wikipedia*: http://en.wikipedia.org/wiki/Jan_Hus).

Many of the educated elite of today are also misleading the masses, ridiculing the Bible, God, and anyone who does not hold on to their unrealistic views.

Many people died horrible deaths to allow everyone access to this book, so why not see whether what they died for has something to offer you (besides a horrible death at the stake).

Then in chapter 11, John hears, "And I will give power to my two witnesses [of God and Jesus Christ], and they shall prophesy one thousand, two hundred and sixty days."

They shall then be killed in Jerusalem at the end of this period, and their dead bodies will lie in the street for three and a half days; after this time, the two witnesses will be resurrected, and a voice from heaven will say to them to come up, and they will ascend up to heaven into a cloud. This happens when Jesus Christ returns to the earth with his angels in the clouds of heaven, and the elect (the chosen ones of Jesus Christ) will also be brought into the returning clouds. In line with a similar account in Paul's letter to the Thessalonians about Christ's return.

Then we who are alive and remain shall be brought up (beamed up) to those who are already in the cloud (the resurrected dead, Jesus Christ, and his angels) in the sky.

The ancient writers inadvertently revealed interactions with beings who have fantastic technology and who claim they can resurrect the dead, even if their bodies have decomposed completely, and make them immortal with new bodies that time and the elements have no effect on.

I would imagine if you have read this book and studied and checked to see whether it is true, you would make the logical assumption that humanity has had interactions with beings of much higher intelligence than ours.

So who are they? Are they aliens from another planet or humans from the future? Who do they say they are?

The Gospel (good news) according to John says, "In the beginning was the Word and the Word was with God. All things were made by him." *The Word* is a title for Jesus Christ, and the statement that he made all things says Jesus was involved in creating the universe.

Genesis 1 says, "In the beginning God created the heavens and the earth...The sixth day, God said, 'Let us make man in our own image, and let him rule over the whole earth.'"

Genesis 2 says, "And the Lord God formed a man out of the dust of the earth [most likely genetic material, such as bone, to make our current species] and breathed into him the breath of life. Then God placed the man in a garden called Eden, in modern-day Iraq. As our creators, they refer to themselves as our father and his son, our older and much-wiser brother. They offer humans the chance to join them as immortals, if we will accept them as such and follow their guidance. That's the primary message in the Gospel (good news). We have the offer of immortality from these beings. As I said in the foreword of *Clouds of the Lord* in the "Old Testament" section.

The clouds of the Lord is only one area of the consistency of the Bible.

Another statement in the Bible says, "I am God and there is none like me, declaring the end from the beginning, and from ancient times things not yet done." The Bible that is in existence today is no amazing coincidence; it was declared from ancient times to reach us today, to give us guidance and hope.

The Bible is full of statements that are similar and for the scoffers, particularly the ones who write these misleading books that state that the Bible is a collection of fables by primitive humans and that anyone who believes it is backward. This one in particular says, "The fool says in his heart 'there is no God,' and by professing themselves to be wise [by writing these misleading books] they have become fools."

I'm not saying this; God did, thousands of years ago. You can believe this book or you can believe the writers of these misleading books. My advice is to make up your own mind. These misleading books actually help to confirm the authenticity of the Bible, which says, "In the last days, scoffers will come, saying, 'Where is he [Jesus Christ]?'" Things go on as they always have.

So if there were no scoffers, then that statement would not be accurate.

These misleading writers inadvertently help to authenticate the Bible. It can be quite hard to believe the Bible without the correct information and the part of the clouds of the Lord, but a thorough investigation reveals time and again the same answer: interaction with supernatural (or superintelligent) beings who ultimately want us to join them as immortals. Perhaps the Bible really is correct, and if it is, it is certainly worth investigating personally. Your choice: investigate, yourself. You do not need to have Harvard or Oxford degrees for this.

When I was at school in the 1960s and 1970s, I was told that the universe is endless and has always existed. Albert Einstein (one of the greatest physicists of all time) believed this to be so in spite of his calculations and genius. When he found out the universe had a beginning and was not static, he called his cosmological constant the biggest blunder of his career.

We now know the universe had a beginning about fourteen billion years ago (the Big Bang) and that everything is travelling through the universe at enormous speed; the earth is travelling through space around the sun at sixty-seven thousand miles per hour.

Everything is moving at terrific speed in all directions away from a central point where the Big Bang occurred approximately fourteen billion years ago. Imagine a balloon being continually inflated to enormous size and that everything in the universe is contained within this balloon.

Genesis 1 says, "In the beginning God created the heavens [universe] and the earth."

The Bible stated thousands of years ago that the universe had a beginning, whereas the intellectual elite of the nineteenth and early twentieth centuries said the universe had no beginning, that it had always been there. Even Albert Einstein fell for this deception, calling it the biggest blunder of his career.

What's at the central point where the universe started? Revelation 20:11 says, "And I saw a great white throne, and him that sat on it, from whom the earth and the heavens fled away."

The earth and the universe are moving quickly away from God, which is to be expected because the creator of the universe, whose throne is at the center of the entire universe yet is outside the universe, created it from there fourteen billion years ago.

There is enormous evidence of design throughout the earth and the entire universe; understanding the role of the clouds of the Lord will help you understand some of the genius of the designers of the earth.

Beings who reveal to us that all creation is our ultimate inheritance for all eternity.

We will not be allowed to conquer the universe till we conquer our defects of character.

The next twenty years will likely culminate in the conclusion of World War III with the deaths of billions of people, as was prophesied in the Bible, and the only thing that will prevent the death of the other billions is the return of Jesus Christ in the clouds of the Lord. The universe awaits us, provided we accept God and Jesus Christ.

CHAPTER 25

SIGNS YET TO COME

Zechariah 14:2 says, "I will gather all the nations to Jerusalem to fight against it; the city will be captured, the houses ransacked, and the women raped. Half of the city will go into exile, but the rest of the people will not be taken from the city."

This is coming over the next decade or two and is a clear sign to understand where we are in Bible prophecy. Half of Jerusalem will be ravished because it will be the Jewish half. The Islamists will get East Jerusalem as their capital, using the pretext that peace will be achieved. When you see Jerusalem (or half of it) taken over by the Islamists, you can rest assured that the time of this prophecy being fulfilled is around the corner.

The horrors of this event will prompt Western intervention. "And at the time of the end the king of the south [Islamic countries are south of Jerusalem] will push at the king of the north; and the king of the north (Russia and Europe are north of Jerusalem) will come like a whirlwind with chariots, and with horsemen and many ships" (Dan. 11:40). This intervention will crush the Islamic war machine, which at that time will be united. After these events occur, Jesus Christ will return in the clouds of the Lord around three years later. Massive armies will cross the Euphrates River in Iraq to attack the Western armies in the Holy Land and its surrounding territories. These armies will be annihilated by Jesus Christ and the returning clouds of the Lord, ushering in real peace world-wide. I know this sounds unbelievable, but it is possible to track these events. Study rigorously what is written in this book, and if you find the past and the present to be accurate and true, you can watch and see the events the Bible predicts occur before your eyes.

CHAPTER 26

666

*"And he causes everyone, both small and great, rich and
poor to receive a mark on their right hand, or in their
foreheads, and made it so no man might buy or sell, except
for the ones that had the mark of the beast, the name
of the beast, or the number of the beast" (Rev. 13:16).
"Here is wisdom, let him that has understanding know
the number of the beast, for it is the number of a man,
and that number is six hundred three score and six"*

(Rev. 13:18).

John wrote down what he saw in a vision as he was commanded
by the resurrected Jesus Christ. Technology beamed images
into his eyes or mind that our science is only starting to embrace
now. John had a vision of today's world, with the financial systems
of the world eliminating cash payments. Many people have been
deceived into coming up with different answers to this, such as 666
tattooed on a child's head as in the omen movies, or a bar code, or

the *B* symbol in bank card. When it came out, it was posted as the 666 of the Bible because the three colored Bs in its emblem looked like three sixes.

John would not recognize the number 666. It did not exist in his time. He recorded what he saw, which looked like six hundred sixty-six, in language that he could understand—and what he saw would be controlling the world's finances in the last days (the last generation of people ruling without God's divine guidance) before Christ's return in the clouds (the same way he left the earth nearly two thousand years ago).

As always, the Bible was correct in predicting a worldwide economic system. This system is now gaining control of the world's finances and eliminating the cash society. By the time Christ returns, it will have full control over the world's finances. Was John a genius who worked out that the entire world would fall into one economic system the way it is heading today? Or did he just record what he was shown would happen, as the book of Revelation states?

Many atheists (who do not have understanding) claim John's writings are either false or delusions. Are we in an age where finances are controlled by a different economic system than in John's day? Of course we are. Was John a genius who independently worked out that financial systems would change so much that the entire world's finances could be controlled by a single entity? That's a big stretch of the imagination. No, John had this revealed to him with vision technology. The banking systems are controlling the entire world's finances more and more. Some of this is a result of the War on Terror and a war on criminal fraud. As time moves along in response to these problems, more and more of the world's finances will be controlled by massive financial companies with trillions of dollars, till we get to the point where no one may buy or sell except under their control.

John saw this nearly two thousand years ago. You don't need to know the exact meaning of the number 666 to be able to see John's prophecy is coming true. (It is really Christ's prophecy. Christ revealed it to John in his old age on the Isle of Patmos, where he had been sent by the Roman authorities.)

Once you understand the real meanings of John's prophecies, the atheists' ridicule falls back on them, making them look like the stupid ones. As the Bible says, "By declaring themselves wise, they have become fools" and "the fool says in his heart there is no God." Do not believe that these experts are experts. If they were such experts, they would have known the significance of the clouds of the Lord. They are actually the fools who declare themselves wise which the Bible prophecies about. The Bible itself warned about these misleading experts coming on the scene thousands of years ago. I hope you have found clouds of the Lord enlightening. I have, writing it in this book. Study and research what is written here, and make up your own mind.